Dhruva: From Silence To Stardom

Preface

The genesis of this story lies in the quiet observation of lives lived, dreams chased, and hearts yearning. It started with a whisper – a fleeting image of a young man, outwardly calm but inwardly burning with an unyielding passion. This quiet intensity resonated with me, sparking a desire to explore the complexities of his journey. Dhruva's story isn't just a tale of ambition and success; it's a poignant exploration of the sacrifices we make, the choices we face, and the enduring power of love, even when it remains just out of reach. My aim was to delve into the emotional landscape of adolescence and young adulthood, where the path to self-discovery is often paved with uncertainty and unexpected twists. The thriller elements woven throughout are not just plot devices; they reflect the inner turmoil and external pressures that Dhruva encounters on his path to achieving his dreams. The suspense is intertwined with his emotional growth, mirroring the unpredictable nature of life itself. This book is a testament to the multifaceted nature of human experience, demonstrating that our journeys are seldom straightforward and our triumphs are often bittersweet. I hope that in reading Dhruva's story, you will not only be entertained but also moved to consider the complexities of your own path, the sacrifices you might make, and the enduring power of your own unique melody. May this narrative resonate with you, prompting reflection and inspiring you to embrace the full spectrum of your own experiences. The journey to self-discovery is seldom linear, and the most compelling narratives often lie in the spaces between the expected and the unexpected.

Introduction

Dhruva's tale unfolds like a carefully orchestrated symphony, blending the soaring highs of triumph with the melancholic depths of unrequited love. His journey begins in the quietude of adolescence, marked by an unassuming exterior that belies a burning ambition. He navigates the treacherous waters of schoolyard teasing, finding solace and strength in an unexpected talent – his voice. This discovery becomes the catalyst for his transformation, propelling him on a relentless pursuit of his dreams. But his path is far from smooth; it's a precarious balance between the demanding pressures of achieving his aspirations and the bittersweet longing for a love that seems perpetually out of reach. This novel explores the potent mix of ambition and sacrifice, showcasing how the relentless pursuit of a goal can both elevate and isolate. Dhruva's narrative is a coming-of-age story infused with suspense, a thrilling exploration of the internal battles waged as he grapples with his identity, his relationships, and the price of success. The suspense elements don't merely drive the plot; they underscore the internal conflicts and external pressures that test his resilience. Each chapter unveils new challenges, new relationships, and new layers to his evolving personality. The narrative is meticulously crafted to build tension, revealing character development alongside escalating conflict, creating a reading experience that is both emotionally resonant and deeply suspenseful. The ending, while satisfying in its resolution, leaves the reader with a lingering sense of the complexities of life, the enduring power of love, and the enduring echoes of choices made.

The Quiet Boys Fury

The air hung thick and heavy in the school hallway, a suffocating blend of stale sweat, cheap disinfectant, and the lingering scent of lunch. Dhruva, small for his age with a perpetually downcast gaze, navigated the crowded corridor, his shoulders hunched as if bearing an invisible weight. He was a ghost, a shadow flitting through the boisterous throng, mostly unnoticed, except by those who delighted in his quietness, his vulnerability. He was the perfect target.

Today, it was Rohan and his gang. Rohan, the alpha of their pack, a hulking figure with a sneer permanently etched onto his face, blocked Dhruva's path, his cronies flanking him like predatory wolves. The fluorescent lights hummed overhead, casting harsh shadows that exaggerated the cruel angles of Rohan's features. Dhruva's heart pounded a frantic rhythm against his ribs, a trapped bird desperate for escape. He felt the familiar prickling of fear, a cold sweat tracing a path down his spine.

"Look what we have here," Rohan drawled, his voice dripping with contempt. "The little mouse. Still scurrying around, are we?" A cruel laugh erupted from his accomplices, echoing through the hallway. Dhruva's fingers tightened into fists, the knuckles turning white. He didn't meet Rohan's gaze, keeping his eyes fixed on the worn linoleum floor, a dull, grey expanse that mirrored the bleakness in his soul.

"Leave me alone," Dhruva mumbled, his voice barely a whisper, lost in the cacophony of laughter.

"Oh, but we can't do that, can we?" Rohan said, his tone laced with amusement. He shoved Dhruva roughly, sending him stumbling against a locker. The metallic clang echoed, amplifying the sense of vulnerability Dhruva felt. He braced himself, expecting the usual barrage of taunts and shoves, the daily ritual of humiliation. But this time, something was different.

This time, the joke went too far.

Rohan's hand shot out, grabbing Dhruva's favorite book—a worn copy of "To Kill a Mockingbird"—from his backpack. The book, a refuge in his lonely world, a source of comfort and escape, was now being used as a weapon. Rohan held it aloft, its pages fluttering like fragile wings, before tossing it into the nearby overflowing trash can.

The sight of his beloved book, crumpled and discarded amongst discarded food wrappers and crumpled paper, ignited a spark within Dhruva. It wasn't just a book; it was a symbol of his quiet refuge, his hopes, and dreams. A wave of nausea washed over him, followed by a searing rage that burned away the years of suppressed anger, fear, and humiliation. The world seemed to sharpen into sharp, vivid focus; the dull hum of the fluorescent lights became a throbbing pulse, and the laughter of Rohan's gang turned into a mocking chorus that clawed at his sanity.

He couldn't breathe. His vision swam, his ears ringing with the echoes of their taunts. For the first time, he wasn't afraid. He was furious. A primitive, primal rage that surged up from the depths of his being, consuming him completely. The quiet, obedient boy was gone, replaced by a force of nature, a hurricane of raw, untamed emotion.

He lunged.

It happened so fast, a blur of motion, a desperate, instinctive reaction. He shoved Rohan, sending him staggering backward. The impact was surprisingly powerful, knocking the wind out of the usually boisterous bully. Rohan's eyes widened in shock, surprise replacing his arrogant smirk. His cronies stood frozen, stunned by this unexpected display of defiance.

Dhruva didn't stop there. He picked up a nearby textbook, the weight of it solid and reassuring in his hand. The fury coursed through him, hot and uncontrollable. He didn't think, he just reacted. He swung the textbook, connecting with Rohan's shoulder with a satisfying thud.

A chorus of gasps erupted from the onlookers. The hallway, moments before alive with laughter, fell into an uneasy silence. Time seemed to slow down, every detail etched into Dhruva's memory: the surprised look on Rohan's face, the wide-eyed fear of his friends, the horrified expressions of the other students.

He had crossed a line. He had unleashed his fury. And it felt... exhilarating.

The bell rang, shattering the silence, the jarring sound pulling Dhruva back from the precipice of his rage. He didn't run; he stood there, chest heaving, the weight of the textbook heavy in his hand. He was trembling, not from fear, but from the aftershock of his explosion. He had felt the surge of power, the intoxicating rush of defiance. It was terrifying and liberating all at once.

The world didn't disappear, though. The consequences would come. He knew that. Suspension, detention, maybe even expulsion. But for the first time, the fear of punishment paled in comparison to the exhilarating freedom he felt, the potent taste of rebellion on his tongue. He had tasted his own power, and it was addictive.

As he walked away, leaving the stunned group behind him, he knew that this was just the beginning. The quiet boy was gone. A seed of rebellion had been planted, and it was already taking root, spreading its tendrils through his soul. The transformation had begun. The quiet boy had found his voice, not in song, not yet, but in a raw, untamed fury that promised a future far removed from the shadows he had once inhabited.

The school grounds seemed different now, almost alien, as if seen through a new lens. The familiar buildings, the manicured lawns, even the ubiquitous smell of freshly cut grass—all felt sharper, more alive, imbued with a newfound intensity. His senses heightened, he noticed details he had never paid attention to before: the way the sunlight slanted through the trees, the vibrant colors of the flowers in the garden, the intricate patterns of the cracks in the pavement.

He walked toward the music room, a place he'd always avoided, a place that held a mysterious allure. He'd heard the faint sounds of music escaping through its closed doors, a symphony of melodies and harmonies that now seemed to beckon him. He paused by the door, a sudden wave of nervousness washing over him. What if he hated it? What if he was terrible? But the thought was quickly replaced by a determination fueled by the residue of the day's events. He needed an escape. He needed an outlet.

He opened the door cautiously. The room was bathed in a warm, golden light, and the air hummed with the vibrations of a piano. A lone figure sat at the keyboard, fingers dancing across the ivory keys, creating a cascade of notes that swirled and soared. It was Mrs. Sharma, the music teacher, a woman known for her gentle demeanor and her passion for music. She looked up as Dhruva entered, a gentle smile gracing her lips.

He stood there, hesitant, not knowing what to say or do. Mrs. Sharma gestured towards an empty chair. "Come in, Dhruva. What brings you here?" she asked, her voice soft and soothing, a stark contrast to the harshness of the day he'd just endured.

He didn't know what to say; his earlier explosive fury had left him drained and emotionally raw. He found himself just standing there, feeling vulnerable and exposed for the first time in a long time.

Mrs. Sharma sensed his turmoil, and without a word, she continued to play. Her music was different now, gentler, more introspective. The melody seemed to weave a story, and in that moment, Dhruva felt a sense of profound peace, a calmness he hadn't known existed. He closed his eyes, allowing the music to wash over him, its soothing notes gradually calming the storm within him.

It was then, as the final notes faded into silence, that he realized he was no longer afraid. He wasn't just the quiet boy anymore; he was more than just the target of bullies. He had discovered a strength he never knew he possessed, and his fury had revealed a path, a possible escape from the pain and the humiliation he had endured for so long. This quiet space, filled with the echoes of music, was his new sanctuary, a place to start again. A place to heal. And perhaps, a place to discover his true voice.

Discovering the Voice

The chipped paint of the practice room peeled like sunburnt skin. Dust motes danced in the single shaft of sunlight slicing through the grimy window, illuminating the worn-out piano keys. It wasn't much, this forgotten corner of the school basement, but it was his. It was a refuge. He'd discovered it by accident, stumbling upon it during one of his habitual escapes from the taunts and shoves that had become the soundtrack of his school life. He'd initially sought shelter from the relentless barrage of mockery, a silent observer in the echoing emptiness. But then, he saw the piano.

His fingers, usually clumsy and hesitant, found the keys almost instinctively. He pressed a tentative chord – a discordant clang that startled him – then another, a little less hesitant this time. The sound resonated through the small space, a fragile echo against the larger silence of his life. It wasn't beautiful; it was clumsy and uncertain, like everything else about him. Yet, in that clumsy sound, he found something else – a release. A voice.

He began tentatively at first, humming melodies born of frustration and loneliness. He didn't know how he knew these tunes, they were less composed and more felt, emerging spontaneously, like a half-remembered dream. His voice, when it finally broke free from the confines of his throat, was surprisingly strong, a deep baritone that resonated with an unexpected power. It surprised even him. He sang of the grey skies and the heavy hearts of his peers, of the loneliness that clung to him like a shadow. He sang of the relentless ache of being unseen, unheard.

He sang of the injustice, of the unfairness he encountered daily. He didn't consciously craft songs of rebellion, but they were there; in every note, in every vibrato, in every wordless cry. It wasn't a polished performance, far from it. His voice cracked, he stumbled over notes, sometimes he forgot the words entirely. But in that imperfection, he found freedom. The room transformed from a desolate hiding place into a sanctuary, a vessel for his unspoken emotions.

The piano became his confidante, a mute witness to his secret triumphs and failures. He spent hours in the basement, the only sounds the rhythmic thump of his fingers on the keys and the raw, unfiltered emotion pouring from his throat. It was cathartic, a physical release of the bottled-up anger, fear, and sadness that had long been suffocating him. The melodies he created were a rebellion against his silent existence, a declaration of his presence, even if it was only to the dusty walls surrounding him.

He discovered a range he hadn't known existed. Sometimes, his voice was a low rumble, a deep growl that spoke of simmering resentment and untapped power. Other times, it soared, a clear, ringing tone that spoke of hope and a yearning for something more. It was a voice as complex and layered as the boy who possessed it. He experimented with different sounds, different rhythms, different textures. He found himself singing in minor keys, notes that captured the bitter undercurrent of his existence, and then, unexpectedly, he'd find himself in major keys, singing of dreams, of possibilities, of a future where the shadows receded and the sunlight bathed him in warmth.

He learned to harness his voice, to control its power, to shape the raw emotion into something beautiful and expressive. He wasn't just singing; he was sculpting. He was creating something tangible from the intangible, something beautiful from the pain. Each song was a step towards self-discovery, a journey of self-expression that liberated him from the constraints of his silent persona.

He began to write his own lyrics, clumsy and raw at first, but slowly becoming more polished, more insightful, more evocative. The words mirrored the turmoil within him, capturing the essence of his silent battles, the quiet desperation, the unspoken rage. He wrote about the weight of expectations, the crushing burden of conformity, and the suffocating silence that surrounded him. He wrote about the things that had been forced upon him, the things he couldn't voice aloud, the things that burned within him.

His songs were about him, his story, a carefully woven tapestry of pain and resilience. He poured his soul into every note, every word, transforming his pain into art. It was a raw, visceral expression of his inner world – a rebellion whispered through music.

One afternoon, as he was lost in a particularly powerful melody, a sound broke the spell. A shuffling sound. He froze, his fingers hovering over the keys, his breath caught in his throat. He held his breath, listening. The sound was close, too close. His heart hammered against his ribs, a frantic drumbeat in the sudden, suffocating silence. The shuffling stopped. A voice, hesitant and low, spoke his name.

"Dhruva?"

He didn't respond, his body rigid with a mixture of fear and apprehension. The voice spoke again, a little louder this time.

"Dhruva, are you in there?"

Fear constricted his throat. He knew that voice. It was Mr. Sharma, the school's stern and unforgiving principal. What was he doing here, in this forgotten corner of the basement? His songs, his rebellion, his secret sanctuary - all of it was suddenly and terribly exposed. He was trapped. The music, once his refuge, now felt like a potential weapon, a possible accusation, a confession. He was caught.

He considered his options, his mind racing. He could stay silent, hoping Mr. Sharma would simply go away, but that seemed unlikely. Or he could confront him, but that seemed even more terrifying. The door handle rattled, and the fear intensified. The squeak of the door hinge was a sharp stab of panic in the confined space. His heart pounded like a war drum. He was caught, exposed, defenseless. The door creaked open, and a single beam of light illuminated the darkness. Mr. Sharma stood in the doorway, silhouetted against the weak light. His expression was unreadable, a mask of sternness.

Mr. Sharma's presence wasn't the angry condemnation he expected. Instead, there was a strange silence, broken only by the faint echo of his own ragged breathing. Then, Mr Sharma simply closed the door behind him and started walking, as if he'd suddenly remembered something more pressing. Mr Sharma slowly made his way toward the piano, the sound of his shoes echoing in the confined space. He stood there for a while, watching Dhruva with a quiet intensity, a silent observer of his rebellion and his quiet strength. A strange question echoed in his mind. Why would Mr Sharma suddenly decide to walk away?

The silence hung heavy between them, thick and suffocating. Dhruva sat frozen, his heart pounding a frantic rhythm against his ribs. He couldn't understand this sudden shift in the atmosphere. The fear that had gripped him moments ago lingered, but now it was overshadowed by a burgeoning curiosity. What would happen next? He had exposed his heart and soul through his music; but would that strength, that voice, become a source of hope or a prelude to disaster? He had no idea, and it was terrifying. Yet, a flicker of something else emerged – a small spark of defiance, of a newfound courage he hadn't known he possessed. His rebellion had begun.

First Taste of Success

The tiny stage of the community hall felt less intimidating now, a familiar friend rather than a looming beast. The nervous flutter in Dhruva's stomach, once a hurricane, was a gentle breeze. He'd performed here before, several times now, each performance chipping away at the shell of shyness he'd carried for so long. The familiar scent of stale popcorn and sweat hung in the air, a comforting aroma associated with his growing success. His voice, once hesitant and thin, had gained strength, resonance, each note now carrying the weight of his emotions, the story of his journey.

Tonight, though, felt different. The energy in the room crackled with anticipation, a palpable hum that vibrated through the floorboards and up into Dhruva's feet. He glanced out at the audience – a sea of faces, some familiar, many new. He spotted Mrs. Sharma, his kind music teacher, her eyes filled with pride. He saw Rohan, the boy who'd once tormented him relentlessly, now watching with an almost awestruck expression. And then, he saw her – Sakshi, nestled in the back row, her presence a silent, powerful force.

His fingers brushed the worn wood of his guitar. The familiar comfort of the instrument soothed his nerves, grounding him in the present. He began to play, his fingers dancing across the strings, weaving a melody that spoke of longing, of hope, of the bittersweet ache of unspoken feelings. His voice, clear and strong, filled the hall, carrying every nuance of emotion. He sang of dreams and aspirations, of overcoming adversity, of the unwavering pursuit of a passion that burned within him.

The applause at the end was thunderous, a wave of sound that washed over him, leaving him breathless. He bowed, a shy smile playing on his lips, the warmth of the audience's appreciation enveloping him like a comforting blanket. This was it – the first taste of real success. It was intoxicating, exhilarating, a feeling he knew he would never forget.

But the sweetness of success was quickly tempered by a bitter aftertaste. After the performance, a man approached him, his eyes narrowed, his smile strained. He introduced himself as Mr. Kapoor, the manager of a well-known local band. He praised Dhruva's talent, his voice laced with a chillingly familiar undercurrent of something else – envy, perhaps, or something far more sinister.

"You've got talent, boy," Kapoor said, his voice low and menacing. "Real talent. But this town's too small for someone like you. You need a bigger stage, a better manager." His words hung in the air, heavy with unspoken threats. Dhruva felt a prickle of unease. This wasn't the supportive encouragement he'd expected. This was something else entirely.

Kapoor's words planted a seed of doubt in Dhruva's mind. Was he truly ready for the next level? Was he naive to believe that his talent alone would pave his way to success? The warmth of the applause faded, replaced by a growing sense of unease. He began to notice other subtle shifts, whispers in the hallways, hushed conversations that abruptly ended when he approached. He caught glimpses of angry stares, faces contorted in a mixture of resentment and jealousy.

The local music scene, once a welcoming haven, now felt like a pressure cooker, simmering with unspoken rivalries and simmering resentment. A new wave of criticism surfaced – anonymous online comments, disparaging remarks veiled as constructive feedback. Some of it was harsh, bordering on cruel. The whispers had morphed into a roar; the undercurrent of threat was becoming a tidal wave of negativity.

One evening, after a particularly successful performance, Dhruva discovered a slashed tire on his motorbike. It was a minor inconvenience, yet it sent a chill down his spine. It was a clear message – a warning. Someone was watching him, someone was not pleased with his progress. The thrill of success was now tainted by a constant undercurrent of fear. He was no longer just a singer; he was a target.

He started to see patterns in the negativity. It always seemed to escalate after a particularly successful performance. It was as if someone was deliberately trying to sabotage his career, to pull him down from the pedestal he had only just begun to ascend. He confided in Sakshi, her concerned eyes reflecting his growing unease. She offered her support, her presence a constant source of strength amidst the growing storm.

But even Sakshi's support couldn't completely dispel the shadow of fear that had begun to consume him. Sleep became elusive, haunted by nightmares of sabotage and violence. The joy he'd once felt in performing was gradually being replaced by a sense of dread, a constant anticipation of the next attack. He started taking precautions, changing his routine, avoiding certain places. He was walking a tightrope, balancing his dreams with a growing fear for his safety.

The anonymous online comments intensified, filled with increasingly personal attacks. He even received threatening phone calls, anonymous voices whispering threats that sent shivers down his spine. The police, initially dismissive, now seemed to take the threats more seriously as the incidents escalated. The comfortable cocoon of success had transformed into a treacherous landscape, full of hidden dangers and lurking enemies.

One night, while rehearsing at a secluded studio, Dhruva discovered tampering with his equipment. The cables were deliberately cut, the microphone was damaged beyond repair. This was no longer a game; this was a clear and present danger. He understood then that the person or people behind these acts weren't just trying to hinder his career, they were trying to hurt him.

The fear was palpable, a suffocating presence that clung to him like a second skin. Yet, even amidst this growing terror, he found a newfound resolve. The seed of rebellion, once a quiet whisper, had grown into a roar. He refused to be intimidated, to be silenced. His music became a weapon, a defiant cry against the forces trying to silence him. He poured his fear, his anger, his determination into his songs, transforming them into powerful anthems of resilience.

The next performance felt different. He stood on stage, not just a singer, but a warrior. His music resonated with a raw, untamed energy, a testament to his resilience, his unwavering spirit. He sang not only for his audience, but for himself, for the voice that refused to be silenced, for the dreams he wouldn't let anyone steal. The applause at the end was even louder, more fervent, a testament to his unwavering strength. It was a victory, not just for his talent, but for his courage, his refusal to succumb to fear. The first taste of success was no longer just about the accolades; it was about overcoming adversity, about emerging stronger from the darkness. His journey was far from over, but this night, he had won a crucial battle. The war, however, had only just begun.

The Shadow of Sakshi

The air crackled with a nervous energy that had nothing to do with the buzzing fluorescent lights of the college cafeteria. Dhruva, perched on a wobbly chair at a table tucked away in a corner, felt it thrumming in his fingertips, a faint vibration mirroring the frantic beat of his heart. He was fiddling with the worn edges of his notebook, the pages filled with lyrics that seemed less inspired and more like desperate pleas. He hadn't felt this unsettled since... well, since before the first time he'd dared to step onto a stage.

He'd chosen this isolated spot deliberately, hoping to avoid the boisterous throng of students — a strategy that had worked flawlessly until a shadow fell across his notebook. He looked up, bracing himself for the inevitable teasing, but the expected jeer never came. Instead, he saw her.

Sakshi.

She was everything he wasn't — vibrant, confident, her laughter a melodic counterpoint to his usual quietude. Her eyes, the color of warm honey, held a spark of intelligence, a mischievous glint that promised adventure. She stood there, radiating an easy grace that made him acutely aware of his own awkward posture, his rumpled clothes.

"Mind if I sit?" she asked, her voice a soft melody that cut through the cafeteria's cacophony.

He stammered, a wordless jumble of syllables escaping his lips before he could collect himself. He nodded, a silent invitation, his cheeks flushing a fiery red. She settled onto the chair opposite him, her presence filling the small space with a warmth that dispelled the nervous chill he'd been carrying.

They talked for hours, it seemed. About music, of course — she played the flute, her fingers dancing across the silver instrument with the same effortless grace she possessed in her movements. He found himself revealing aspects of himself he usually kept carefully hidden — the insecurity beneath the newfound confidence, the fear that his success was fleeting, a phantom he couldn't quite grasp. He spoke of his dreams, his anxieties, the bittersweet ache of his ambitions. To his astonishment, she listened, not with pity, but with an understanding that resonated deeply within him.

She talked about her own aspirations, her dreams, her fears, not in hushed tones of vulnerability, but with a defiant spirit that both captivated and slightly intimidated him. She wasn't afraid to be herself, unapologetically bold and intelligent, a stark contrast to the hesitant, self-conscious boy he had been just months ago.

Their conversations were a kaleidoscope of shared laughter and intense silences, punctuated by the clinking of cutlery and the murmur of other students. He felt a connection with her, a pull he couldn't quite explain, a sense of belonging he'd never experienced before. It was exhilarating and terrifying all at once. He felt safe with her, yet a knot of apprehension tightened in his chest.

The seed of rebellion that had sprouted within him during his arduous journey to musical stardom now seemed to blossom anew, a rebellious flower pushing through the fertile soil of his newfound emotions. His quiet obedience was dissolving, replaced by an urgent need to reach out, to connect, to share the whirlwind of emotions that were consuming him.

But there was a shadow lurking, a subtle disquiet that shadowed their budding connection. He sensed a fragility in their connection, a potential for heartbreak that resonated with the unspoken anxieties in their shared silence. The shadow of his rising fame fell between them, a subtle but palpable barrier. His world was expanding, filled with adoring fans, thunderous applause, and the intoxicating allure of success. But in this whirlwind of achievement, he was losing a sense of himself.

He saw the apprehension in her eyes, a flicker of doubt behind her usual radiant smile. He knew that his world, his relentless pursuit of musical perfection, was a world she couldn't readily inhabit. The chasm between their worlds, though not yet gaping, was already widening.

One evening, as they sat by the college lake, the moon a silvery disc hanging heavy in the inky sky, he confessed his fears. He spoke of the demands of his career, the endless tours, the suffocating pressure to maintain his image, the loneliness that clung to him like a persistent shadow even amidst the throngs of cheering crowds. He was afraid of losing her, of sacrificing the one genuine connection he'd found in his tumultuous climb to the top.

She listened patiently, her hand resting gently on his, offering a silent comfort that was more potent than any spoken words. He saw a hint of sadness in her eyes, a reflection of his own anxieties.

"I understand," she said, her voice soft but firm. "But don't let fear steal your joy. Your music… it's incredible, Dhruva. It touches people. Don't let anything extinguish that fire."

Her words were a balm to his wounded spirit, a reassurance that he wasn't alone in his struggle. Yet, even as he felt a surge of relief, the shadow lingered, a constant reminder of the precarious balance of their relationship. He knew, with a chilling certainty, that their journey together would be far from easy. The path ahead was paved with potential pitfalls, the sharp edges of ambition and fame threatening to tear them apart.

The following weeks were a blur of rehearsals, concerts, and stolen moments with Sakshi. He was living a double life – the celebrated singer, adored by millions, and the ordinary young man desperately clinging to a love that felt both precious and fragile. He juggled his demanding schedule with late-night talks by the lake, trying to capture those fleeting moments of normalcy before the whirlwind of his career swept him away again.

He noticed a change in Sakshi, a subtle shift in her demeanor. The vibrant sparkle in her eyes sometimes dimmed, replaced by a thoughtful, pensive gaze. He knew she was grappling with his demanding career, the ever-increasing distance between them.

One night, after a particularly grueling concert, he found her waiting for him backstage. The usual radiant smile was absent, replaced by a determined set to her jaw.

"Dhruva," she began, her voice hushed, laced with an undercurrent of tension. "We need to talk."

The words hung in the air, heavy with unspoken anxieties. He knew, instinctively, that this conversation would change everything. The seed of rebellion had grown into a sapling, strong and resilient, but vulnerable to the winds of fate. His journey, already fraught with challenges, was about to take a dramatic and unpredictable turn. The shadow of his success had fallen not only between them but was threatening to eclipse their love entirely. His heart pounded in his chest, a frantic drumbeat against the silence that had descended upon them. This was not just a conversation; it was a battle, the first significant conflict in a war for his heart and his future. The fight for Sakshi, for their fragile love, had begun.

Choosing the Path

The weight of the unspoken hung heavier than the humid air of the Delhi evening. Sakshi's face, usually alight with a mischievous sparkle, was clouded with a worry that mirrored his own. He'd confessed his ambition, his burning desire to sing, to dedicate his life to the music that pulsed through his veins, a life that stood in stark contrast to the structured, predictable path his parents had meticulously laid out for him – a path leading to a secure, respectable career in engineering.

He'd seen the flicker of disappointment in her eyes, the subtle shift in her posture, the way her fingers unconsciously tightened around her coffee cup. It wasn't anger, not exactly. It was a quiet understanding, laced with a fear that resonated deep within his own soul. The fear of losing her. The fear of failure. The fear of choosing a path that might lead to nothing but shattered dreams and a life lived in the shadow of what could have been.

"I… I don't know what to say, Dhruva," Sakshi finally whispered, her voice barely audible above the low hum of conversation in the crowded café. The clinking of cutlery and the murmur of voices seemed to amplify the silence between them, creating a vacuum that threatened to swallow them whole.

He reached across the small table, his fingers brushing against hers. The contact sent a jolt of electricity through him, a stark reminder of the connection that bound them, a connection he wasn't sure he could risk jeopardizing.

"I know," he said, his voice rough with emotion. "It's a lot. It's... everything."

The truth was, it was everything. His singing wasn't just a hobby; it was an integral part of who he was, a burning passion that consumed him, a voice that yearned to be heard. To abandon it would be to silence a part of himself, to deny the very essence of his being. Yet, to pursue it meant risking everything he held dear – his family's approval, his secure future, and, most importantly, Sakshi.

The pressure mounted, a vise squeezing the air from his lungs. He thought about his parents, their faces etched with the expectation of a life meticulously planned, a life that didn't include the uncertainty of a musical career. He saw their disappointment, the subtle disapproval in their eyes, the unspoken words that hung between them like a suffocating blanket. He knew they meant well, they wanted him to have a comfortable, stable life, shielded from the harsh realities of a world where talent didn't always translate into success.

He glanced at Sakshi, her eyes searching his, seeking reassurance, seeking an answer that he himself didn't possess. The decision was a labyrinth, a complex web of possibilities, each path promising both reward and ruin. He could choose the safe route, the predictable path, the one that would please his parents and ensure a secure future. But that path, he realized with a chilling certainty, would lead to a life devoid of passion, a life lived in muted tones, a life where the vibrant melody of his soul would forever remain unsung.

Or, he could take the leap of faith, embracing the uncertainty, the risk, the potential for failure. He could choose the path of his dreams, a path that might lead to glory, to recognition, to a life filled with the electrifying energy of his music. But that path, he also knew, could lead to heartbreak, to disappointment, to a life lived in the shadow of regret. And it could cost him Sakshi.

The image of his family flashed in his mind - his mother's gentle smile, his father's firm handshake, their unwavering love. He imagined their disappointment, the unspoken words, the subtle judgment that would inevitably follow his decision. Then, he pictured Sakshi, her radiant smile, her infectious laughter, the warmth of her touch, the way she made him feel alive. The fear of losing her, of shattering the bond they shared, was a weight he couldn't ignore.

Days bled into weeks, each filled with the agonizing process of weighing the options. The weight of his decision pressed down on him, a constant companion, a shadow that followed him everywhere. He found himself losing sleep, his dreams a chaotic jumble of soaring melodies and crashing disappointments. His appetite waned, his energy depleted, his once bright eyes now clouded with a persistent weariness. The vibrant energy that had once fueled his singing now felt choked, stifled by the weight of his indecision.

He spent hours practicing, pouring his heart and soul into his music, seeking solace in the notes, the rhythms, the harmonies. The music became his refuge, his sanctuary, a place where he could escape the turmoil of his thoughts, where he could find a momentary peace amidst the chaos.

He tried to talk to his parents, but the conversation felt stilted, fraught with unspoken tensions. Their concern was evident, but their understanding remained elusive. They saw his passion, but they couldn't comprehend the depth of his desire, the burning intensity of his ambition. They couldn't see beyond the risks, beyond the uncertainties, beyond the potential for failure. Their love was undeniable, but their acceptance was conditional.

He attempted to discuss his dilemma with his closest friends, but their advice was as fragmented and uncertain as his own thoughts. Some urged him to follow his dreams, to chase the elusive path of passion. Others cautioned him against the risks, reminding him of the stability and security of a traditional career. Their opinions only served to amplify his internal conflict, leaving him more confused and uncertain than ever before.

One evening, sitting alone in his room, surrounded by his instruments, Dhruva found himself confronting the most daunting truth. The path he chose would not only dictate his future but would also shape his relationship with Sakshi. He knew that pursuing his singing career would demand sacrifices, long hours of practice, rigorous touring schedules, and the constant pressure to perform. The life of a singer was far from stable; it was unpredictable, demanding, and unforgiving.

He imagined Sakshi, patiently waiting for him, her love unwavering, despite the challenges he faced. But he also imagined the strain that his demanding career would place on their relationship, the long periods of separation, the jealousy, the misunderstandings, and the potential for resentment. The music he loved might come between them, separating him from the very person he most desired to be with.

The choice was a cruel one, a test of his resolve, a trial of his ambition. Would he choose the comfort of the predictable path, sacrificing his dreams for the sake of stability and love? Or would he risk everything, throwing himself into the unpredictable world of music, potentially losing the person he cherished most in the process? The answer, he knew, lay not in the logic of reason, but in the depths of his own heart, in the resonance of his soul. The seed of rebellion, planted long ago, had finally blossomed, forcing him to confront the most crucial decision of his life, a decision that would define his future, for better or for worse. The silence in the room was broken only by the gentle hum of his guitar, a silent testament to the turmoil raging within him. The path lay before him, clear and distinct, yet fraught with peril. Which path would he choose? The question hung heavy in the air, unanswered, a challenge only he could face.

The Grind

The air in the practice room hung thick with the scent of sweat and anticipation. Dhruva, barely eighteen, was a whirlwind of motion, his body a conduit of raw energy channeled into precise movements. Each note he sang was a testament to the countless hours spent honing his craft, each breath a carefully calculated risk. The worn-out floorboards creaked a mournful rhythm under his restless feet, a soundtrack to his relentless pursuit of perfection. He wasn't just practicing; he was carving out his future, note by agonizing note.

The walls, once bare, were now plastered with inspirational quotes, scribbled lyrics, and Polaroids capturing fleeting moments of progress – a testament to the grueling climb. His reflection in the cracked mirror showed a young man transformed. Gone was the shy, perpetually bullied boy; in his place stood a leaner, more intense version, his eyes burning with a fierce determination that mirrored the fire in his voice. The quiet boy's fury, the seed of rebellion from his past, had bloomed into something potent and unstoppable.

His days were a blur of vocal exercises, rigorous rehearsals, and the endless search for the perfect song. Sleep was a luxury he could rarely afford, sacrificing rest for practice, for the relentless pursuit of his dream. He lived on instant noodles and lukewarm coffee, fueled by the sheer force of his ambition. His phone, perpetually buzzing with messages from hopeful promoters and dismissive agents, lay forgotten in a corner, a testament to his solitary dedication.

The grind was brutal. There were days when his voice gave out, his throat raw and aching, the notes escaping him in ragged gasps. There were days when doubt gnawed at him, whispering insidious lies of failure and inadequacy. He would stand before the mirror, staring at his own reflection, searching for a flicker of hope amidst the growing despair. But then, he would remember the cruel laughter, the stinging humiliation of his past, and a surge of anger would propel him forward, silencing the doubts with a renewed intensity. The past was his fuel, the fire that kept him burning through the long nights and the even longer days.

His repertoire wasn't limited to simply singing; he was meticulously crafting his stage presence, studying every nuance of his movements, his expressions, his gestures. He watched countless videos of his idols, dissecting their performances, analyzing their techniques, searching for inspiration and refining his own unique style. He was a sculptor, painstakingly chiseling away at the raw material of his talent, shaping it into a masterpiece.

His apartment, a tiny, cramped studio above a bustling bakery, was a reflection of his life – organized chaos, a testament to his dedication. Scores lay scattered on the floor, coffee stains marking the rhythm of his sleepless nights. Empty energy drink cans formed small towers, silent witnesses to his tireless efforts. The small kitchen table, usually littered with unfinished assignments and forgotten meals, was now the impromptu headquarters for his burgeoning career. Here, amidst the stacks of sheet music and half-eaten sandwiches, he built his kingdom, one note at a time.

He wasn't alone in this struggle. A small, but fiercely loyal, group of friends offered unwavering support, their belief in his talent as unwavering as his own ambition. They were his anchor, grounding him amidst the storm of his aspirations. They were the ones who would share his meager meals, his cramped living space, his dreams, his doubts, and his occasional moments of triumph.

These were his silent cheerleaders, celebrating his successes, offering comfort during his setbacks, their camaraderie a vital lifeline in the isolation of his self-imposed exile. They understood the sacrifices he was making, the hours he was sacrificing, the compromises he had to make, all for the pursuit of a dream so audacious that it bordered on the impossible.

But even amidst the unwavering support of his friends, a constant undercurrent of anxiety ran through his life. The fear of failure was a shadow that stalked him, a relentless companion, its presence a constant reminder of the precariousness of his situation. He knew that the odds were stacked against him; the music industry was a brutal battlefield, filled with cutthroat competition and broken dreams. Many had started where he was, but only a select few ever made it to the heights he so desperately yearned for.

His voice, once a refuge, now felt like a burden, a heavy responsibility. It was a magnificent instrument, capable of breathtaking beauty and soul-stirring power, but it was also a source of intense pressure, a constant reminder of the expectations weighing upon his shoulders. The fear of letting down his friends, his supporters, and most of all, himself, intensified with every passing day, fueling his already intense dedication.

There were times he questioned his own sanity, the toll his ambition took on every aspect of his life. He pushed himself relentlessly, ignoring the physical and emotional exhaustion that clung to him like a second skin. He was a tightrope walker, balancing precariously between success and failure, with the potential for a devastating fall ever-present in his mind.

Despite the ever-present threat of failure, Dhruva persisted, driven by an unwavering belief in his own potential. He knew that the path to success was paved with setbacks and disappointments, but he was also aware that the rewards of his labor would far outweigh the sacrifices he was making. Each challenge, each setback, only strengthened his resolve, sharpening his focus and deepening his determination. He wasn't merely chasing fame or fortune; he was chasing a dream, and this dream was his lifeblood.

His dedication was contagious. It inspired those around him, fueling their own ambitions and inspiring them to pursue their own dreams with equal fervor. The positive energy he exuded, a manifestation of his inner strength, permeated through every aspect of his life, affecting everyone who came into contact with him. This created a unique energy around Dhruva, drawing others into his orbit, creating a loyal following before he even achieved significant mainstream success.

Even amid the relentless grind, moments of unexpected joy pierced through the intensity of his efforts. The simple act of sharing a laugh with his friends, or the thrill of a small victory, provided the necessary respite, reaffirming his purpose and fueling his tireless pursuit of his dream. These were the moments that reminded him of the humanity at the heart of his journey, of the shared experience of striving, of the unwavering bonds of friendship, and the unwavering support that made this arduous journey possible. These were the moments that kept him going, that prevented him from being completely consumed by the demanding nature of his chosen path.

His relationship with Sakshi, though strained by his relentless pursuit of his career, remained a constant source of both inspiration and anxiety. The brief encounters, stolen moments, and whispered promises fueled his determination, reminding him of what he was working for, of the life he hoped to build, one where he could share his success with the one person he cherished most. But the distance, the missed calls, and the unspoken anxieties created an additional layer of suspense in his life, a constant reminder of the sacrifices demanded by his ambitions. The delicate balance between his dreams and his love for Sakshi was a tightrope he walked daily, the potential for a devastating fall ever present. His journey, far from being solely about the attainment of his goals, was an intricate dance between ambition, sacrifice, and the enduring power of love. The suspense lay not only in his success, but also in his ability to maintain the balance, to hold onto the things that truly mattered while chasing his elusive dreams.

Early Victories Growing Pains

The first local gig felt like a baptism by fire. The smoky haze of the dimly lit pub clung to Dhruva's throat, a stark contrast to the pristine air of his practice room. The microphone felt heavy, unfamiliar, amplifying the tremor in his hands. The crowd, a blur of faces illuminated by flickering stage lights, seemed a million miles away, yet their energy pulsed, a palpable current he could almost taste. He launched into his song, a melody born from years of solitary practice, and the silence that followed his opening notes felt like an eternity. Then, the music took over, a wave carrying him forward, silencing the doubts that clawed at his mind. The applause at the end was deafening, a tidal wave of sound that washed over him, leaving him breathless and exhilarated. It wasn't the grand stage of his dreams, but it was a victory, a tiny crack in the wall of his aspirations.

This initial success spurred him onward. He played smaller venues, absorbing the lessons each performance offered – learning to command the stage, to connect with the audience, to channel his emotions into every note. Each gig, each positive review, fueled his ambition, confirming his belief in himself, in his talent. He started garnering a small but dedicated following, people who recognized the raw talent and the unyielding passion that vibrated in every performance. He began to feel the thrill of the chase, the intoxicating pull of success. It was addictive, the rush of the stage lights, the roar of the crowd, the validation of his hard work.

But the path to success wasn't a straight line. There were moments of self-doubt, nights when his voice failed him, when his nerves betrayed him, leaving him stranded in the spotlight, feeling utterly exposed. There were harsh criticisms, whispers of inadequacy that haunted him in the quiet of his room. He learned to push through these moments, to use the setbacks as fuel, to transform his anxieties into a driving force. He learned that even the most talented individuals face adversity, that success was not a destination but a relentless journey, a constant process of refinement and growth.

One particularly brutal setback came in the form of a regional talent competition. Dhruva had poured his heart and soul into preparing for this competition, seeing it as a springboard to larger stages. He'd meticulously chosen his song, practiced tirelessly, and visualized his victory. The anticipation was palpable, a thick, suffocating blanket of nerves that clung to him during the weeks leading up to the event.

The competition itself was a whirlwind of emotions. The stage was larger, the lighting brighter, the atmosphere charged with a palpable tension. He saw his competitors, some polished and professional, others brimming with raw energy— a diverse group of young musicians, all hungry for success. He felt a flicker of apprehension, a whisper of doubt in the midst of his carefully constructed confidence. His performance was good, technically flawless, but something felt...off. He lacked the fiery passion that usually ignited his performances, his voice missing its usual vibrancy. The judges' expressions were inscrutable, their silence more daunting than any outright criticism.

The announcement of the winners was a stark contrast to the excitement of the competition. His name was not called. The disappointment was crushing, a lead weight in his chest, silencing his very core. The reality of his failure, the stark contrast between his ambition and the reality of his defeat, hit him hard, leaving him feeling lost and vulnerable. He'd poured everything into this competition, sacrificing countless hours, pushing himself to the limits of his physical and mental endurance. The silence of the auditorium seemed to amplify the intensity of his failure. It was more than just a loss; it was a brutal lesson in the fickle nature of success.

He retreated to his practice room, the familiar sanctuary offering little solace. The silence was oppressive, amplifying the sting of defeat. The weight of his failed ambition bore down on him, suffocating his spirit. He questioned his talent, his dedication, his entire career path. He'd placed all his eggs in this one basket, and now, the basket lay shattered at his feet. The path to success, once a seemingly bright trajectory, now felt treacherous and uncertain.

Days blurred into a haze of self-doubt and introspection. He struggled to find the motivation to pick up his instrument, the joy of music replaced by a heavy sense of disillusionment. His usual routine – the rigorous practice sessions, the meticulous preparation – felt pointless, a futile attempt to recapture the lost energy and confidence. He found himself isolated, withdrawing from his friends and family, consumed by the turmoil within. The silence of his room echoed his inner turmoil, a deafening reminder of his failure.

The turning point came unexpectedly, during one of his quiet, self-imposed solitary sessions. He wasn't trying to practice or rehearse, but simply allowing himself to feel the overwhelming weight of his emotions. He sat with the quiet melancholic tunes, letting the melody pour over him. And in the midst of his despair, a spark flickered. He realized that the competition wasn't the measure of his worth. It was a setback, yes, a painful and humbling one, but it wasn't the end. He still possessed his talent, his passion, his unwavering determination.

He began to see his failure not as a defeat, but as a critical step in his journey, a crucial moment of learning and growth. He started to practice again, this time with a renewed sense of purpose, a clearer understanding of his path, a newfound resilience that had been forged in the fires of his disappointment. His approach changed. He began to focus on refining his craft, honing his skills, and experimenting with new musical styles. The competition had provided a valuable lesson; he wouldn't let another setback define him. He knew that success was not just about winning competitions but about constantly refining his craft and connecting with his audience.

This newfound resilience manifested itself in his next performance. He was invited to a small festival, a chance encounter that could have easily been dismissed after his previous failure. But this time, he approached the stage with a quiet confidence, a sense of purpose that emanated from within. He poured his heart and soul into his performance, transforming his earlier disappointment into a raw and powerful energy that resonated with the audience. The performance was a testament to his tenacity, a triumph not just over his recent setback, but over the self-doubt that had threatened to consume him. The applause at the end felt different, richer, more meaningful, fueled not just by talent but also by resilience.

The festival performance led to other opportunities, each one a building block in his growing career. He began to attract the attention of music industry professionals, people who recognized his talent, his passion, and the story woven into every note he sang. He started receiving invitations to larger venues, each one a step closer to his dream. He began to encounter competition, rivals vying for the same spotlight, each with their own unique talents and ambitions. This competition, unlike the regional talent show, fueled him, sharpened his focus, pushing him to refine his craft and to explore the full potential of his voice. The undercurrent of rivalry added a thrilling edge to his journey, transforming the pursuit of success into a game of skill, strategy, and perseverance. He felt the growing pressure, the constant need to improve, to surpass expectations, to stay ahead of the game. This fueled his ambition and enhanced his determination, transforming him into a more confident and capable artist.

He started to understand the intricacies of the music industry, learning to navigate the complexities of contracts, recordings, and marketing strategies. He learned that success wasn't solely about talent; it demanded a fierce determination, resilience, and an understanding of the business side of the industry. He started making tough choices, balancing his artistic vision with the demands of commercial success. It was a complicated tightrope walk, a constant negotiation between his artistic integrity and the pressures of the industry, an ongoing challenge that added suspense and thrill to his journey.

His early victories had been significant, but they were just the first steps on a long and winding road. The growing pains were numerous, each one a lesson in perseverance, resilience, and the importance of remaining true to himself, even in the face of relentless pressure and the relentless pursuit of success. The future promised greater challenges, fiercer competition, and the inevitable risks that accompany such ambitious aspirations. But Dhruva was prepared. He had faced failure and emerged stronger, more determined, and more driven than ever before. He was ready for whatever came next.

The Price of Fame

The roar of the crowd was a physical force, a wave that crashed over Dhruva, leaving him breathless and exhilarated. His first major stadium concert was a blur of lights, sound, and thousands of faces all turned towards him. The feeling was intoxicating, a potent cocktail of adrenaline and validation. He'd dreamt of this moment, envisioned it countless times in his quiet practice room, but the reality exceeded all expectations. It was a triumph, a testament to years of relentless dedication, of sacrifices made, of dreams chased with unwavering focus.

But the dizzying heights of fame came with a price. Suddenly, he was no longer just Dhruva, the boy who'd once been teased for his quiet nature. He was Dhruva, the rising star, a name whispered in hushed tones, plastered across magazine covers, a face recognized in every corner of the globe. His life transformed overnight. The anonymity he'd once cherished was replaced by constant attention, a relentless spotlight that followed him everywhere. The simple act of walking down the street became an ordeal, a gauntlet of flashing cameras and outstretched hands. He learned to navigate the throngs of fans and paparazzi with a practiced ease, a carefully constructed persona designed to shield him from the overwhelming intensity of his newfound fame.

His relationship with Sakshi, already fragile, began to unravel under the strain. The distance, both physical and emotional, widened with each passing day. His schedule, a relentless cycle of rehearsals, recordings, interviews, and concerts, left little room for anything else. He tried to maintain contact, to make time for her, but the demands of his career were relentless, a constant, inescapable pull. He'd send her messages, late at night, between sound checks and interviews, apologies for his absence, promises to call, promises he rarely kept. He watched her grow distant, the spark in her eyes dimming, replaced by a quiet sadness that mirrored his own. His phone calls became shorter, less frequent, his responses more hurried. The guilt gnawed at him, a constant, low hum of regret. He knew he was losing her, drifting apart, and the knowledge felt like a cold hand closing around his heart.

The loneliness was pervasive, a chilling companion in the opulent world he now inhabited. His lavish apartment, once a symbol of success, felt more like a gilded cage. He was surrounded by people, yet profoundly alone. The constant noise, the flashing lights, the endless stream of conversations, all served only to amplify the silence within him, a silence that echoed with the absence of the one person who truly understood him. He longed for the simple days, the quiet evenings spent with Sakshi, the shared laughter, the comfortable silences, the intimacy that now seemed a distant memory.

His professional life thrived amidst this personal turmoil. He won awards, his songs topped the charts, his concerts were sold out in minutes. The critics praised his voice, his talent, his stage presence. He was lauded as a prodigy, a musical genius. The world seemed to be at his feet, a kingdom built on the foundation of his extraordinary talent. But the weight of this success pressed down on him, a burden he carried with a weary grace. He performed, he smiled, he posed for the cameras, a flawless façade that hid the turmoil within. The cheers of the crowds, once a source of immense satisfaction, now felt hollow, a distant echo in the cavern of his loneliness.

The relentless pursuit of perfection took its toll. The pressure to maintain his image, to meet the impossible expectations of his fans and critics, became suffocating. Sleepless nights were spent agonizing over minor imperfections in his performances, replaying past concerts in his mind, searching for flaws where none existed. He drove himself relentlessly, pushing his limits to the breaking point, fueled by a fear of failure that gnawed at his soul. He knew that one slip-up, one minor misstep, could shatter his carefully constructed world, sending him tumbling back into the anonymity he had so desperately escaped.

The constant scrutiny of the media added another layer to his torment. Every aspect of his life was dissected, analyzed, and judged. His relationships were scrutinized, his past excavated, his every move dissected and analyzed in the relentless pursuit of a story, a scandal. He learned to navigate the treacherous currents of public opinion, to manage his image, to control the narrative. He became a master of deception, a chameleon who shifted and changed to suit the demands of his public persona.

The pressures of fame also strained his relationships with his family and friends. His parents, initially overjoyed by his success, found it difficult to connect with the man their son had become. The gulf between them widened, filled with unspoken resentments and misunderstandings. His old friends, once his confidantes, struggled to keep up with his whirlwind life, their attempts at casual conversations often interrupted by the insistent calls of his managers and the demands of his publicist. He tried to maintain his connections, to nurture the relationships that had once been so important, but time and distance worked against him, eroding the bonds that once held him together.

One evening, after a particularly grueling concert tour, he found himself alone in his apartment, surrounded by the ghosts of his past. The silence was deafening, the weight of his success a crushing burden. He looked at his reflection in the darkened window, a stranger staring back at him, his eyes haunted, his expression weary. He felt an overwhelming sense of emptiness, a void that all his fame and fortune could not fill. He reached for his phone, the impulse to call Sakshi overwhelming, but he hesitated. The fear of rejection, of hearing her voice filled with indifference or resentment, paralyzed him. He let the phone slip from his grasp, the silence of his apartment swallowing him whole. He was at the pinnacle of his career, the best singer in the world, yet his victory felt hollow, a stark reminder of the price of fame. The price he had paid, and the price he continued to pay, for the elusive dream of success. He knew, deep down, that something had to change, that the journey to true fulfillment lay beyond the glittering facade of his celebrated life. The path ahead remained uncertain, shrouded in the shadows of his past and the weight of his present. But the quiet resolve to find his way back, to find something beyond the fleeting applause and the hollow victories, began to stir within him. The journey had just begun, a new chapter yet unwritten.

Sakshi's Distance

The phone lay cold and inert on his nightstand, a stark contrast to the burning ache in his chest. He hadn't called Sakshi. He couldn't. The thought of her voice, even the imagined sound of her laughter, felt like a cruel taunt, a reminder of everything he'd sacrificed, everything he'd lost in the relentless pursuit of his dream. The stadiums roared, the crowds chanted his name, yet the silence in his own life was deafening.

He scrolled through his phone, a gallery of pictures a morbid testament to a life lived in two distinct realities. One: the dazzling world of sold-out concerts, flashing cameras, and adoring fans. The other: a handful of blurry photos of Sakshi, captured during stolen moments, memories fading like ink in water. He remembered her face, etched in his mind with the same clarity as the lyrics to his most popular song. But even that clarity felt tainted, blurred by distance and unspoken words.

Their last conversation was a jumble of hurried sentences and rushed goodbyes. He'd promised to call, promised to visit, the words tumbling out in a desperate attempt to bridge the chasm that was growing between them. Promises that echoed now, empty and hollow, like the applause that faded moments after the final note.

The weight of his absence pressed down on him, heavy as a lead blanket. He pictured her, somewhere, living her life, moving on. The thought sent a shiver down his spine, colder than the November rain lashing against his windowpane. He imagined her with someone else, a someone who had the time, the energy, the presence that he so callously squandered on his ambition. Jealousy, a bitter, unfamiliar emotion, clenched at his heart. This wasn't the triumph he'd envisioned.

His career soared, propelled by a force he barely understood. Each concert was a step further away from her, each award a heavier weight on his conscience. He received countless messages of admiration, declarations of love from strangers who felt a connection to his music, his pain, his vulnerability. But none of those messages filled the void left by Sakshi's absence. None of it mattered, not truly. He traded intimacy for adoration, real connection for the fleeting high of a stadium full of screaming fans.

He tried to find her online, a desperate attempt to glimpse a part of her life, to know if she was happy, if she missed him. He found nothing. Her social media was devoid of anything personal, a carefully constructed wall against the prying eyes of the world. He wondered if that wall was also built against him.

The guilt was a constant companion, a shadow that followed him onto the stage, into the recording studio, even into his dreams. He saw her face in the faces of his fans, a haunting reminder of the human connection he'd sacrificed. He sang about love, about loss, about longing, his voice carrying the weight of his unspoken regrets. The irony wasn't lost on him. His songs became his confession, his lament, a public display of a private agony.

He tried to compensate, to make amends. He sent her flowers, anonymous gifts, each a silent apology, a desperate plea for forgiveness. They went unanswered. The silence was deafening, more profound than the roar of any crowd he'd ever faced. He knew, instinctively, that material gestures wouldn't suffice. He needed to be there, to speak to her, to look into her eyes and beg for a second chance. But the fear held him back, the fear of rejection, of hearing the finality in her voice, the confirmation of his failure.

One night, after a particularly draining tour, he booked a flight, a reckless, impulsive decision fuelled by desperation. He landed in her city late at night, the city lights a blurry kaleidoscope through his tired eyes. He drove to her apartment building, the familiar address a beacon in the darkness. He sat in his car, watching her building, a silent observer of her life from a distance. The lights flickered on and off, a rhythm that echoed the chaotic beat of his heart. He saw a figure move in the window, a shadow, a fleeting glimpse of what might have been.

He didn't go up. He couldn't. The courage he possessed on stage, the confidence that captivated millions, deserted him in the face of this personal confrontation. He sat there until dawn, the silence broken only by the distant city hum. He watched the sun rise, painting the sky in shades of gold and orange, a breathtaking scene that offered little comfort. He felt defeated, broken, the weight of his ambition crushing him, the gap between his public persona and his private despair wider than ever before.

The flight back was a blur. He arrived home, his apartment feeling colder, emptier than ever. His awards sat on the shelves, gathering dust, silent witnesses to his hollow victory. He realized that he'd climbed to the top of the world, only to find himself utterly alone. He had achieved his dream, but at what cost? The price of fame, he now understood, was more than he'd ever bargained for. It was a price measured in lost connections, missed opportunities, and a heart burdened by a silence far louder than any applause.

The emptiness gnawed at him, an insistent ache that no amount of success could alleviate. He wondered if he could ever truly forgive himself. He wondered if Sakshi would ever forgive him. And in the quiet solitude of his opulent apartment, he realized that his journey, far from being over, had just begun—a journey not towards further acclaim, but towards a redemption that seemed impossibly distant, a reconciliation that felt as elusive as the melody of a forgotten song. The path to true fulfillment, he understood, lay not in the deafening roar of the crowd, but in the quiet whispers of a heart yearning for connection, a heart longing for forgiveness, and a heart desperately seeking the lost love of Sakshi. His next song, he knew, would be a different kind of ballad entirely; a song of regret, a song of longing, and perhaps, a song of hope. But hope, he realized, was a fragile thing, a delicate bloom that needed careful nurturing, a bloom that might never blossom in the shadow of his past mistakes. The road ahead was long and arduous, but he would walk it, one step at a time, toward a future that could only be as bright as he allowed it to be.

A Defining Performance

The air hung thick with anticipation, a palpable tension that vibrated through the floorboards of the grand concert hall. Thousands of faces, a sea of expectant eyes, stared back at Dhruva from the darkness. He stood backstage, the roar of the crowd a muted rumble, a distant echo compared to the tempest raging within him. This wasn't just another concert; this was the "Phoenix Rising" tour, his biggest yet, his most ambitious undertaking. This was a defining performance, a chance to solidify his place at the apex of the music world. But more than that, it felt like a trial, a judgment, a reckoning.

He gripped the microphone stand, the cold metal a strange comfort against the clammy sweat on his palms. The weight of expectation pressed down on him, the unspoken pressure of proving himself, not just to the screaming fans, but to himself. Could he truly live up to the hype? Could he, after all the years of relentless work, the sacrifices, the compromises, deliver a performance worthy of the moment? The doubt, a venomous serpent, coiled in his gut, threatening to suffocate him.

The stage manager's voice, a crisp, reassuring tone cutting through the pre-show chaos, broke through his thoughts. "Five minutes, Dhruva."

He took a deep breath, trying to regulate the erratic rhythm of his heart. His mind raced, replaying every note, every lyric, every movement of his upcoming performance. He had poured his soul into this album, "Phoenix Rising," a collection of songs that reflected his journey – the pain, the struggle, the triumph, and the lingering ache of his unfulfilled love for Sakshi. Each note held a piece of his heart, a fragment of his story.

He walked onto the stage, the blinding spotlight momentarily stealing his breath. The roar of the crowd hit him like a physical wave, a sonic tsunami that threatened to drown him. But this time, it was different. This wasn't the deafening roar that had once been a source of comfort, a confirmation of his success. This was a challenge, a test of his mettle.

He began to play, the opening chords of "Broken Wings" echoing through the vast hall. His voice, usually a powerful instrument capable of filling stadiums, started tentatively, a fragile whisper against the surging energy of the crowd. This vulnerability, however, was intentional. He wanted to share the rawness of his emotions, the vulnerability that lay beneath the surface of his carefully constructed persona.

The song unfolded, building intensity with each verse. He channeled the pain of his past, the regret, the longing, into his voice. He sang about the sacrifices he'd made, the dreams he'd chased, and the price he'd paid. He sang about Sakshi, her absence a palpable presence in the music. The crowd, initially stunned by the unexpected vulnerability, was captivated. The silence between the verses was charged with unspoken empathy, a shared understanding of the universal language of heartbreak.

As the song progressed, his voice grew stronger, more confident. The initial fragility transformed into a powerful anthem of resilience. He sang not just of pain, but of hope, of the phoenix rising from the ashes of his past mistakes. He sang of redemption, of forgiveness, of the possibility of a brighter future. The crowd responded, their silence replaced by a thunderous applause, a wave of support that washed over him, cleansing him of his self-doubt.

The performance continued, each song carefully selected, a tapestry woven from threads of raw emotion and soaring melodies. He moved through the set, his movements fluid and expressive, his energy infectious. The crowd was mesmerized, completely absorbed in his performance. He could feel their energy, their enthusiasm feeding his own.

But it wasn't just the technical prowess, the powerful vocals, or the carefully choreographed movements that resonated with the audience. It was the authenticity, the rawness of his emotions, that transcended the stage and connected with the hearts of thousands. They saw in him not just a talented singer, but a man grappling with the complexities of life, a man who had stumbled and fallen but had risen to face his challenges.

Midway through the concert, a hush fell over the crowd. He launched into a new song, a ballad he had written only recently, a song he had never performed before. The notes, melancholic yet hopeful, hung in the air, each chord weaving a tale of love lost and love found. He sang of forgiveness, of acceptance, of the bittersweet joy of second chances.

As the final notes faded, a profound silence filled the hall, a silence broken only by the occasional sniffle or suppressed sob. The audience was moved, deeply affected by the emotional rawness of his performance. The emotion was so real, so palpable that it hung in the air like a thick fog. This wasn't just a concert; it was a cathartic experience, a shared moment of vulnerability and connection.

Then, the applause erupted, a wave of sound that shook the very foundations of the building. It wasn't just polite clapping; it was a roar of appreciation, a testament to the power of his music, the depth of his emotions, and the

unwavering courage he had shown in sharing his
vulnerabilities with the world.

The encore was a whirlwind of energy, a joyous celebration
of his triumph. He felt the love of the audience washing over
him, a tide of support that carried him to the end of the
performance. He left the stage, exhausted but exhilarated,
knowing that this performance had been a turning point, a
moment that would define his future.

He had faced his fears, bared his soul, and emerged stronger,
more resilient, more authentic than ever before. The Phoenix
had indeed risen. But the journey was far from over. The
applause faded, replaced by the quiet hum of the cooling
lights and the faint whispers of the departing crowd. Alone
once again, the weight of his past still lingered, a constant
reminder of the sacrifices he'd made. The victory felt
incomplete. The roaring success tasted like ashes in his
mouth.

He had achieved the pinnacle of his musical career. The
world celebrated his talent, his voice. But he knew, with a
sickening certainty, that the true song of his life, the melody
of complete fulfillment, remained unsung. The love he
longed for, the connection he craved, still eluded him, a
haunting reminder of the compromises he'd made along the
way.

Back in his hotel room, the silence was deafening. The
cheers and applause of the audience were distant echoes,
fading memories. The emptiness returned, a constant
companion in the gilded cage of his success. He picked up
his phone, his fingers hovering over Sakshi's number. He
hesitated, the fear of rejection a cold hand on his heart. He
knew the call wouldn't erase his past mistakes, wouldn't
magically fix the broken pieces of his life. But it might be a

start, a step towards the true redemption that he craved, a first note in the symphony of a life he hoped to rebuild, a life where success and happiness weren't mutually exclusive. He closed his eyes, took a deep breath, and finally pressed the call button. The phone rang, the sound a nervous tremor against the silence of his opulent room. The future, he knew, was uncertain. But for the first time in a long time, he felt a flicker of hope. The rising sun painted the cityscape in hues of orange and gold, a subtle promise of a new dawn. The phoenix had risen, but its flight had only just begun. His journey, he realized, was far from over.

Global Recognition

The roar of the crowd was a physical thing, a wave crashing over him, lifting him higher and higher. Confetti rained down like a blizzard of celebratory snow, each tiny piece a testament to his triumph. Dhruva, bathed in the blinding glare of the stage lights, felt a strange disconnect. The cheers, the applause, the adoration – it was all a surreal spectacle, a dream he'd worked tirelessly to achieve, yet now that he was here, at the pinnacle of his career, a chilling emptiness gnawed at him. He was the best singer in the world, a title whispered in awe in every corner of the globe, yet the taste of victory was bitter, leaving a residue of loneliness in its wake.

His life had transformed beyond recognition. The cramped, cluttered apartment he shared with his parents had been exchanged for a sprawling penthouse overlooking the city. His once-modest wardrobe was now filled with designer clothes, his travel itinerary a whirlwind of international flights and five-star hotels. Fans swarmed him wherever he went, their faces blurring into an indistinguishable sea of adoring eyes. He signed autographs until his hand cramped, posed for countless photos until his smile felt strained, and gave interviews until his voice was hoarse. The relentless demands of fame were a relentless tide, threatening to pull him under.

He had chased this dream with a fierce, almost desperate intensity. Every sacrifice, every sleepless night, every stinging rejection had fueled his ambition, driving him further and further towards this seemingly impossible goal. He'd imagined this moment countless times, envisioned the triumphant feeling of success, the satisfaction of proving everyone who doubted him wrong. But the reality was far more complex, far less satisfying.

The weight of expectation was crushing. Every performance felt like a high-stakes gamble, a constant test of his ability to maintain the flawless image the world had projected onto him. One misstep, one off-key note, one moment of vulnerability could shatter the carefully constructed facade. He felt the pressure mounting with each passing day, the fear of failure a constant companion, a shadow lurking just behind his every breath. The joy had long since faded, replaced by a gnawing anxiety that kept him awake at night.

His relationships suffered under the strain. His family, though proud of his accomplishments, felt distant, their lives irrevocably altered by his meteoric rise. His friends, once close and familiar, seemed to fade away, their lives diverging from his orbit, their voices becoming muffled by the cacophony of fame. He yearned for the simple days, for the easy camaraderie, for the unburdened laughter that now felt like a distant memory.

And then there was Sakshi. The memory of her, the lingering scent of her perfume, the echoes of her laughter – they were a phantom limb, a constant ache in his heart. His pursuit of fame had come at a heavy cost, a price paid in lost connections and unfulfilled dreams. The distance between them had grown into a chasm, an unbridgeable gap created by his relentless pursuit of his ambition. He often wondered what could have been, what their life might have looked like if he had chosen a different path, if he hadn't let his ambition eclipse his personal life.

New faces filled his days – glamorous women, powerful executives, shrewd managers – each adding a layer of superficiality to his life. Their fleeting connections offered temporary solace, brief escapes from the crushing weight of his isolation, but they left him emptier than before, their charm proving as hollow as the accolades thrown at him from every direction. He felt like a stranger in his own life, a chameleon adapting to the shifting demands of his environment, but always feeling fundamentally alone.

One evening, while staring out at the glittering cityscape from his penthouse, a wave of nausea washed over him. The city that once symbolized freedom now felt like a gilded cage. His reflection in the glass seemed unfamiliar, a stranger in expensive clothing, a vacant smile plastered across his face. He saw the emptiness in his own eyes, a haunting mirror reflecting his hollow victory.

The next morning, he sought refuge in an old, dusty box hidden in the corner of his storage room. Inside, he found a collection of old photographs. His younger self stared back at him - the shy boy from his childhood, the one who had discovered his gift in the confines of his small town, the one filled with dreams and unbridled joy. He picked up a crumpled note, a faded letter from Sakshi, one he'd tucked away, preserved as a relic from a time before fame had consumed him. Tears welled up in his eyes, a release of pent-up emotions.

He felt an overwhelming urge to escape, to break free from the confines of his carefully constructed world. He longed for the simplicity of his past life, for the genuine connection he'd shared with those who knew him before the world knew him. He decided then and there to step back, to recalibrate, and to finally confront the bitter truth of his success.

He started slowly, cancelling interviews and turning down lucrative offers. He began to rediscover the music he loved, not for the applause but for the sheer joy of creating. He used his newfound free time to search for Sakshi, driven by a burning need to reconnect, to mend the shattered fragments of their relationship.

He tracked her down, to a small town far away from his world, a place filled with the tranquility that his life desperately needed. He found her working as a teacher, a life far removed from the glitz and glamour of his career. Their reunion was filled with both trepidation and anticipation. The years apart hadn't erased the affection between them, but they had etched lines of caution onto their faces.

Their conversation was slow and deliberate, each word carefully chosen, a testament to the distance they'd had to bridge. Dhruva confessed his regrets, his realization that fame was a fleeting thing, a poor substitute for the simple joys of genuine connection. He revealed the hollow emptiness of his success, how the deafening roar of the crowd couldn't fill the void left by her absence.

Sakshi listened patiently, her eyes revealing a blend of understanding and sadness. She admitted that she had missed him, that the memory of their early days had always lingered. But she also spoke of the sacrifices she had made, the life she had built, the wounds his pursuit of fame had inflicted. Their conversation left many questions unanswered, many bridges still unbuilt.

The future remained uncertain, the path ahead still shrouded in shadow. But as he looked into Sakshi's eyes, Dhruva felt a flicker of hope, a promise of a future where success didn't have such a bitter taste. The journey back wouldn't be easy, but for the first time in a long time, he felt a sense of purpose, a direction in his life that extended beyond the confines of his career. He knew his victory was far from complete, but the journey towards a more fulfilling life had begun. The taste of success remained bitter, but he was finally ready to find the sweetness that lay hidden beneath.

The Weight of Expectations

The relentless pursuit of perfection, fueled by the intoxicating elixir of global acclaim, had begun to warp Dhruva's perception of reality. The adulation, initially a source of overwhelming joy, now felt like a suffocating blanket. Every performance was a high-stakes gamble, each note weighed down by the crushing weight of expectation. The fear of failure, once a distant whisper, had grown into a monstrous roar in his mind, a constant companion lurking in the shadows of his success. His meticulously crafted public persona, the charming, effortless singer, was beginning to fray at the edges, revealing a darker, more fractured self beneath.

Sleep became a luxury he could barely afford. The endless cycle of interviews, photo shoots, and concerts bled into one another, a dizzying blur of flashing lights and deafening applause. His days were measured in the relentless march of deadlines, his nights haunted by the specter of impending disappointment. He found himself increasingly reliant on stimulants, the caffeine fueling his exhausted body while the ever-present anxiety gnawed at his soul. The vibrant energy that once propelled him forward was now a flickering flame, threatened by the chilling winds of self-doubt.

His relationships suffered. Sakshi, the ever-present anchor in his life, felt increasingly distant, a ghost at the periphery of his existence. His attempts at communication were clumsy, stilted, his words failing to bridge the chasm that had grown between them. He longed for the simple intimacy they once shared, the unspoken understanding that had defined their connection, but the relentless demands of his career had choked the life out of their relationship. The weight of his success had driven a wedge between them, a silent testament to the sacrifices he had made on the altar of ambition.

The pressure extended beyond his personal life. His management team, once his allies, now felt like jailers, their concern morphing into a suffocating control. Every decision, every public appearance, every social media post was meticulously scrutinized, every move dictated by the insatiable hunger of the entertainment machine. He was no longer Dhruva, the boy who dreamed of singing; he was a brand, a commodity, carefully packaged and marketed to a global audience. The authenticity that had once defined his music was being slowly eroded, replaced by a carefully curated image designed to maximize profits and maintain his carefully constructed illusion of perfection.

He found himself retreating further into himself, the vibrant, mischievous spirit that had once characterized him fading into the background. The witty banter he once enjoyed now felt like a performance, a carefully calculated act designed to appease his audience. His laughter felt hollow, his smiles strained, the mask he wore in public slipping only in the quiet solitude of his hotel rooms. The silence, once a source of peace and creativity, now felt like a suffocating vacuum, amplifying the anxieties that gnawed at his soul.

One evening, backstage after a particularly grueling concert, he found himself staring at his reflection in a cracked mirror. The face that stared back was gaunt, the eyes shadowed with exhaustion, the lips drawn tight with an almost imperceptible tremor. A stranger stared back at him, a reflection of the toll his relentless pursuit of success had taken. The carefully constructed persona had cracked, revealing the fragile man struggling to hold it together beneath the surface.

The following days were a blur. The strain became unbearable. He missed concerts, cancelled interviews. His team, alerted by the sudden absence of the meticulously crafted Dhruva, grew frantic. They'd seen this coming. The pressure cooker environment they themselves had created had finally begun to boil over.

The whispers started. Speculations filled the tabloids. Was he having a breakdown? Was his career over before it truly began? The very success that had defined him was now threatened by the darkness that had taken root within his soul. He was trapped in a spiral of self-destruction, the weight of expectations crushing him beneath its unrelenting force. His carefully constructed reality was crumbling, revealing the vulnerabilities and insecurities he'd desperately tried to hide beneath the veneer of effortless charm and unparalleled talent.

He sought solace in unexpected places. He started spending more time in secluded parks, surrounded by the quiet rustling of leaves and the gentle murmur of a nearby stream. The anonymity of these spaces provided a momentary respite from the relentless scrutiny of his public life. He rediscovered the simple joys of life – the beauty of a sunlit afternoon, the feel of grass beneath his bare feet, the tranquility of watching clouds drift lazily across the sky.

But the shadows persisted. The memories of past failures, long buried beneath layers of success, resurfaced, whispering insidious doubts in his ear. He relived moments of self-doubt, the harsh criticisms of early audiences, the agonizing practice sessions that pushed him to his limits. The weight of expectation, once external, now felt profoundly internalized, a relentless voice that condemned him for his imperfections.

In the quiet moments, between the frantic pace of his public life, he began to question everything. His ambition, once a beacon guiding him toward his dreams, now felt like a cruel mistress, demanding endless sacrifices without offering commensurate reward. The glittering prize of global recognition seemed tarnished by the bitter taste of loneliness, the hollow ache of unfulfilled desires. The success he'd so diligently pursued had left him empty, bereft of the very things he valued most – genuine human connection and inner peace.

He sought professional help, a brave step born from desperation and a fragile flicker of self-awareness. The therapist's office was a stark contrast to the dazzling world of concerts and interviews, a sanctuary where he could shed the mask of perfection and confront the anxieties gnawing at his soul. He began to understand that his success wasn't a measure of his worth, that his value wasn't tied to his public image. The journey to self-acceptance was long and arduous, a slow and painful process of peeling back the layers of self-deception and confronting the vulnerabilities he'd hidden for so long.

The road to recovery was not linear. There were setbacks, moments of profound despair when the weight of his past failures threatened to overwhelm him. Yet, with each session, with each small step towards self-understanding, a glimmer of hope emerged, a renewed sense of purpose that transcended the confines of his career. He began to reconnect with the music, rediscovering the passion that had initially ignited his journey. The songs he wrote reflected his struggles, his vulnerabilities, his journey towards healing. The raw emotion resonated with his audience in a way that his carefully crafted earlier work hadn't, creating a deeper connection that transcended mere entertainment.

The bitter taste of success had been a harsh teacher, but in its crucible, Dhruva discovered a strength and resilience he never knew he possessed. He was still the best singer in the world, but he was also something more – a survivor, a man who had stared into the abyss and emerged stronger, wiser, and more profoundly connected to himself and the world around him. The journey was far from over, but for the first time in a long time, Dhruva looked to the future with a sense of cautious optimism, ready to embrace the challenges ahead, not as a burden but as an opportunity for growth, for healing, and for a more authentic expression of his true self. The weight of expectations remained, but it no longer crushed him; it challenged him, pushing him to discover a depth of strength he never knew he possessed.

New Temptations

The private jet hummed, a metallic lullaby against the backdrop of the pre-dawn sky. Below, the world was still cloaked in darkness, a stark contrast to the dazzling world Dhruva inhabited. He stared out the window, the city lights a glittering tapestry spread across the inky canvas. Success had painted his life in vibrant, almost unreal hues, but the colors were starting to blur, the edges softening into a hazy uncertainty.

His latest album had shattered sales records, a testament to his relentless pursuit of perfection, a relentless pursuit that had left him hollowed out, a shell of the vibrant young man he once was. The constant touring, the endless interviews, the suffocating pressure to maintain his image – it all felt like a gilded cage. He'd traded the quiet solitude of his childhood for a life of relentless public scrutiny, a life where authenticity was a rare commodity.

The tour brought him to Milan, a city of romance and art, a stark contrast to the sterile environments of recording studios and concert halls he had become accustomed to. Here, the air hummed with a different kind of energy, a vibrant pulse that resonated with a part of him he thought he'd lost. He found himself drawn to the hidden corners of the city, the cobblestone streets echoing with the ghosts of centuries past, the aroma of freshly brewed espresso hanging heavy in the air. It was a balm to his weary soul, a temporary reprieve from the relentless demands of his fame.

It was during one such exploration that he met Isabella. She was a painter, her eyes reflecting the same intensity and passion he once poured into his music before it became a commodity. She didn't know who he was, not at first. She saw him, not as Dhruva, the global singing sensation, but as a man lost in thought, a man searching for something he couldn't quite name. Their conversations flowed effortlessly, fueled by a shared love of art, of life, of the hidden beauty found in the everyday.

Isabella challenged him, her questions cutting through the carefully constructed facade he'd built around himself. She questioned his music, probing beneath the surface of the polished melodies, searching for the raw emotion that had once fueled his passion. Her insights were sharp, unsettling, forcing him to confront the emptiness that had taken root within him. He found himself revealing parts of himself he'd kept buried deep, confiding in her his anxieties, his fears, his loneliness.

The intimacy of their conversations, the shared vulnerability, was intoxicating. It was a stark contrast to the superficial relationships he'd cultivated in the whirlwind of his career. The women he had met, drawn to his fame and fortune, sought a connection with the persona he presented to the world, not the man he was behind the polished veneer. Isabella saw through the carefully crafted illusion.

One evening, walking along the banks of the Naviglio Grande canal, Isabella's hand brushed against his. The contact sent a jolt through him, a spark of something he hadn't felt in years, a connection that transcended the superficial. It was a moment of intense vulnerability, a surrender to a feeling he'd consciously avoided, a feeling that threatened the carefully constructed equilibrium of his life.

The connection with Isabella sparked a dangerous internal conflict. Part of him craved the simplicity of their relationship, the genuine connection that cut through the

superficiality of his fame. Yet, another part, deeply
entrenched in the world of his success, recoiled from the idea
of jeopardizing everything he'd worked so hard to achieve.
The thought of sacrificing his career, his carefully
constructed image, terrified him.

The next few weeks were a blur of stolen moments,
clandestine meetings in hidden cafes, late-night walks along
moonlit canals. The passion between them was undeniable, a
fiery intensity that threatened to consume him. But the
knowledge that his world, the world of global tours and sold-
out stadiums, was incompatible with this newfound intimacy,
cast a dark shadow over their budding romance.

He found himself torn between two worlds, two very
different lives. On one hand, the glittering world of fame and
fortune, a world that demanded his unwavering attention and
left him feeling increasingly empty. On the other, the quiet
intimacy of his connection with Isabella, a world that offered
genuine connection, but threatened to unravel the carefully
constructed tapestry of his life.

His record company, sensing a shift in his demeanor, a subtle
change in his creative energy, grew increasingly anxious.
They saw the risk in his newfound emotional vulnerability, a
risk that could potentially damage his carefully crafted
image. They started to subtly pressure him, reminding him of
the demands of his career, the financial stakes involved in
maintaining his position at the pinnacle of the music
industry.

The pressure intensified, mirroring the internal struggle he
was experiencing. His agent, a shrewd and ruthless
businessman, hinted at the consequences of neglecting his
career, the potential loss of endorsements, the risk of losing
his devoted fanbase. The weight of those consequences

pressed down on him, a chilling reminder of the price of his success.

One evening, after a particularly draining concert, Isabella confronted him. She had seen the strain in his eyes, the internal conflict that raged beneath the surface. She saw the fear, the uncertainty, and the weight of expectation that clung to him like a second skin. Her words were gentle, yet direct, cutting through the carefully constructed facade he had erected around himself.

She reminded him of the passion that fueled his music in his early days, a passion that had been gradually extinguished by the relentless pursuit of success. She questioned whether his fame had become a prison, a gilded cage that confined him to a life devoid of genuine connection.

Her words hit him like a tidal wave. He realized she was right. He had sacrificed so much for his career, trading personal happiness for global recognition. He had become a prisoner of his own success.

The choice was stark, a brutal dichotomy between the life he'd built and the life he truly craved. He could continue down the path he'd chosen, sacrificing his soul for the fleeting glory of fame, or he could risk it all for the chance at something real, something true, something that filled the void that had grown within him.

The decision, while agonizing, felt inevitable. The bitter taste of success, the loneliness it brought, the superficial relationships it forged, was a constant reminder of the sacrifices he'd made. It was in that moment, standing alone under the Italian stars, with the weight of his decision pressing down on him, that Dhruva knew what he had to do.

The road ahead would be fraught with uncertainty, a path leading away from the dazzling lights of fame and into the unknown. But as he looked into the vast expanse of the night sky, he felt a sense of peace he hadn't experienced in years. The choice wasn't easy. But it was his. And for the first time, he felt truly free. The future was uncertain, yet for the first time, the unknown felt less like a threat and more like an invitation. A chance to finally rewrite his story, on his own terms.

Haunted by the Past

The hum of the jet engines faded as Dhruva stepped onto the tarmac, the crisp morning air a shock to his system after the recycled air of the cabin. He inhaled deeply, the scent of jet fuel strangely comforting, a familiar smell that linked him to this surreal life he now led. The flashing cameras momentarily blinded him, a sea of faces blurring into an indistinguishable mass. He offered a practiced smile, a mask he'd perfected over years of navigating the treacherous waters of fame. But behind the smile, a chill ran down his spine. It wasn't the cold; it was the memory, a ghost from his past, whispering in his ear.

The memory surfaced unbidden, a vivid tableau from his childhood. He was ten, maybe eleven, huddled in the alley behind his school, the reek of stale garbage clinging to the air. A group of older boys circled him, their taunts sharp as shards of glass. He remembered the burning shame, the helpless rage simmering beneath his skin, the silent vow he'd made to never again feel so powerless. That vow, fueled by resentment and a desperate need to prove himself, had driven him to the relentless pursuit of his dream. His singing, his escape, had become his weapon, his shield, his ultimate revenge.

But the victory felt hollow. The roar of the crowd, the adulation of millions, couldn't silence the echoes of those taunts. The bitterness lingered, a persistent taste on his tongue, even as champagne bubbles fizzed on his palate at celebratory events. Success had given him a platform, a voice that resonated across continents, but it hadn't healed the wounds of his past. The fear, the vulnerability, still lurked beneath the surface, a constant shadow that danced at the periphery of his triumph.

He pushed the memory away, focusing on the present. His manager, a sharp-dressed woman with eyes that missed nothing, approached. Her smile was tight, professional. "The press conference is in fifteen minutes," she said, her voice clipped. "They're eager to hear about your upcoming world tour."

The press conference was a blur of flashing lights and shouted questions. He answered with practiced ease, delivering the rehearsed responses with a carefully cultivated air of nonchalance. But inside, the ghost of his past continued its relentless assault. He saw the reflection of his eyes in the lens of a camera – eyes that held a depth of sadness that no amount of makeup or carefully crafted image could conceal. He was a master of illusion, a puppeteer pulling the strings of his public persona, but the strings themselves were frayed, worn thin by the weight of his buried emotions.

Later, alone in his hotel room, the illusion crumbled. The meticulously crafted façade fell away, revealing the raw, vulnerable boy who'd once cowered in that alley. He sank onto the plush, king-sized bed, the silk sheets offering little comfort. He closed his eyes, and the memories flooded back, sharper, more vivid than ever before.

He recalled the sleepless nights spent practicing, his voice raw and aching, his fingers bleeding from gripping the microphone too tightly. He remembered the sacrifices he'd made, the friendships forfeited, the relationships sacrificed at the altar of his ambition. He thought of Sakshi, her face a fleeting vision in his mind's eye, her laughter echoing in the silence of his opulent suite. His success hadn't brought him closer to her; it had driven them further apart. The distance between them felt insurmountable, a chasm carved by time, ambition, and unspoken words.

The loneliness gnawed at him, a relentless beast feeding on his deepest insecurities. He was at the pinnacle of his career, a global superstar, yet he felt profoundly alone. The applause, the adoration, the wealth – none of it filled the emptiness within. He was haunted, not by the ghosts of the past, but by the choices he'd made, the paths he'd chosen to tread in his desperate quest for validation.

A knock at the door startled him. He hesitated, his heart pounding in his chest. He wasn't used to visitors, preferring the solitude that had become his constant companion. He opened the door cautiously, expecting to see his manager or a member of his team. Instead, he saw a woman he hadn't seen in years, a woman who had been an integral part of his past – his former music teacher, Mrs. Sharma. Her face was etched with worry, her eyes filled with a mixture of concern and understanding.

"Dhruva," she said softly, her voice laced with an emotion he couldn't quite decipher. "I heard about your concert. You were magnificent."

Her words, though meant as praise, struck him as strange, somehow out of place. The compliment, unexpected in its sincerity, hit him harder than the scathing criticism of his early years. He invited her in, his guarded demeanor momentarily forgotten. He watched as she took in his luxurious surroundings – a stark contrast to the humble beginnings they both shared.

Mrs. Sharma saw the turmoil in his eyes, the pain masked by the carefully constructed façade of success. "I know this life isn't easy, Dhruva," she said, her voice gentle. "Fame comes at a price."

He poured her a glass of water, his hands trembling slightly. He confessed, not knowing how, but feeling compelled to let the years of pent-up emotions spill out. He spoke of the bullying, the relentless pursuit of his dream, the sacrifices, the emptiness that lay beneath the glittering surface of his success. He confessed about Sakshi, the unfulfilled love that cast a shadow over his achievements. He talked of the lingering bitterness, the haunting memories that refused to let go.

Mrs. Sharma listened patiently, her gaze unwavering. When he had finished, she placed her hand gently on his arm. "You've achieved so much, Dhruva," she said, her voice filled with a quiet strength. "But success shouldn't come at the cost of your peace. Your journey isn't over. It's just beginning. There is still time to heal, to mend the wounds of your past, and to find the happiness you deserve."

Her words were a balm to his soul, a soothing counterpoint to the relentless cacophony of his inner turmoil. He looked at her, seeing not just a former teacher but a beacon of hope in the darkness that had enveloped him. The ghost of his past hadn't vanished, but its grip loosened, the haunting whispers becoming a faint murmur rather than a deafening roar. The bitterness, though still present, tasted a little less sharp, the edges softened by the unexpected empathy and validation. He realized that his journey to success was only half the story. The other half, the more challenging part, was the journey back to himself – a journey of healing, self-acceptance, and a renewed search for genuine happiness, one that extended far beyond the stage lights and the roar of the crowd. The road ahead was still uncertain, but for the first time, the weight of his past seemed bearable, the journey ahead less daunting. He had a long way to go, but he finally had a compass to guide him.

Sakshis Reappearance

The limousine ride from the airport was a blur of flashing lights and muffled shouts. Dhruva, cocooned in the plush leather, felt strangely detached, his usual sharp senses dulled by a wave of exhaustion and a persistent, low-level anxiety. The success he'd craved, the life he'd meticulously built, felt hollow, a gilded cage that trapped him rather than liberated him. The memory of Mrs. Sharma's words, her gentle understanding, was a fragile lifeline in this sea of manufactured glamour.

He arrived at his penthouse apartment, a sprawling sanctuary overlooking the city, yet it felt more like a prison. The silence, broken only by the low hum of the air conditioning, was deafening. He needed to unpack, to settle in, but the simple act felt monumental, a task too overwhelming for his weary soul. He sank onto the plush sofa, the soft cushions offering little comfort. His phone buzzed, a relentless stream of messages and calls from his management team, demanding his attention, his time. He ignored them, the insistent vibrations a discordant symphony against the silence in his heart.

Days bled into weeks. The relentless schedule of rehearsals, interviews, and performances was a blur. He moved through his days in a haze, a sleepwalking automaton, performing his role with practiced ease but feeling utterly disconnected from the adulation and the applause. He was a ghost, a phantom haunting his own life. The emptiness within him gnawed at him, a relentless hunger that success couldn't satiate.

Then, one evening, a simple email shattered the monotony. A single line, barely visible amidst the deluge of spam and promotions, stopped him cold: "It's me, Sakshi." His breath hitched. He reread the email, the simple words echoing in his mind, a seismic shift in the landscape of his carefully constructed world. His heart pounded a frantic rhythm against his ribs, a mixture of hope and fear.

His hands trembled as he typed a reply, his fingers hesitant, unsure. He wrote simply, "I... I need to see you."

The meeting was arranged for a small, unassuming café tucked away in a quiet corner of the city. He arrived early, his nerves a tangled mess, his carefully constructed composure crumbling under the weight of anticipation. He ordered a black coffee, the bitter taste familiar, mirroring the complexity of his emotions. He watched the entrance, every passing face a potential disappointment, every movement a surge of adrenaline.

Then he saw her.

Time seemed to stop. Sakshi hadn't changed much. Her eyes, still bright and intelligent, held a depth that years of distance hadn't erased. A hesitant smile played on her lips as she approached, a cautious hope mirroring his own. She looked stunning, even more radiant than he remembered. The years had only enhanced her beauty, adding a maturity and a quiet confidence that was both alluring and intimidating.

He stood, his chair scraping against the tiled floor, the sound deafening in the sudden hush that fell between them. The air crackled with unspoken words, with years of regret, longing, and unspoken feelings. Her eyes met his, a silent acknowledgment of the passage of time, of the paths they'd chosen and the distance they'd traveled.

"Dhruva," she said, her voice soft, a gentle whisper that cut through the silence.

He simply nodded, unable to speak, the words trapped in his throat, choked by the weight of emotion. The years of separation melted away, replaced by the raw, unfiltered connection he had so desperately tried to suppress. He saw in her eyes a reflection of the turmoil he carried within himself, a shared understanding of the sacrifices they'd both made.

They talked for hours, the café emptying around them, the silence of the night punctuated only by their whispers. She spoke of her life, her studies, her dreams. He spoke of his music, his career, his relentless pursuit of success. It wasn't a simple confession of love, but a weaving of two lives, a tapestry woven with threads of loss, of regret, and of a lingering hope. The bitterness he had carried for so long began to subside, replaced by a fragile, tentative sense of understanding.

Sakshi didn't criticize his ambitions, didn't chastise him for his choices. Instead, she listened, offering her empathy, her understanding. She spoke of the sacrifices she had made, too, the dreams she'd put aside, the life she'd envisioned that had never come to pass. The weight of their shared experiences bonded them, a shared burden that eased the pressure of individual regrets.

He learned she had been traveling, broadening her horizons, searching for a direction, a purpose. She spoke of working with underprivileged children, her passion for music transforming into a desire to nurture young talent. The passion in her voice moved him more than any adulation he had ever received.

He finally understood. His success had been a solitary pursuit, fueled by ambition and a desperate need for validation. He'd climbed the mountain, reached the peak, only to find himself alone, staring out at an empty landscape. Sakshi's reappearance wasn't just a romantic reconciliation, it was a revelation. A pathway to a life beyond the stage lights, beyond the pressures of fame. It was a chance to redefine success, not just as a measure of achievement but as a journey of growth, a pursuit of genuine connection.

The conversation wasn't without its painful moments. The hurt, the unspoken words, the missed opportunities—these were ghosts that still lingered between them. But the pain was tempered by a newfound understanding, a recognition of the shared responsibility for the distance that had grown between them. The silence between them was different now, imbued with a deeper connection, a shared history that held both sorrow and hope.

He confessed his regrets, his constant yearning for her, a longing that had shaped his career, his persona, even his failures. He admitted that his ambition had blinded him, that he had chased success at the cost of everything else that mattered, including her.

Sakshi listened patiently, her eyes never leaving his. There was no judgment, only understanding. She confessed her own regrets, her own pain. She admitted she had loved him deeply, a love that had shaped her life, even in his absence. She had carried a piece of him within her heart, a silent devotion that had never truly faded.

As the first rays of dawn painted the sky, they walked out of the café, the city waking around them. The weight of years of unspoken words and missed opportunities lifted slightly, replaced by a tentative hope, a fragile sense of possibility.

The future was still uncertain, their path unclear. But for the first time in a long time, Dhruva felt a flicker of genuine happiness, a warmth that extended beyond the fleeting applause of a crowd. The bitter taste of success had finally begun to yield to a sweeter, more profound flavor – the hope of a love rediscovered, a future rebuilt, and a sense of self that was no longer solely defined by the music he made, but by the connections he formed. He felt a sense of peace he hadn't experienced since he was a boy, a peace that surpassed the thrill of sold-out stadiums and chart-topping albums. It was the quiet peace of a heart finally finding its way home. He had a long journey ahead, but he had Sakshi by his side, and that made all the difference.

A Confrontation

The biting New York wind whipped around Dhruva, mirroring the turmoil inside him. He hadn't felt this cold, this exposed, since he was a boy, huddled in the schoolyard, the jeers of his classmates echoing in his ears. Now, years later, standing on the precipice of a career that had once seemed like a shimmering, unreachable star, he felt that same chilling vulnerability. The success, the adulation, the sold-out stadiums – it all felt like a fragile, glittering illusion, poised to shatter at the slightest touch.

He stared at the reflection in the darkened window of his penthouse apartment, the city lights blurring into an indistinct, shimmering haze. The face staring back was different – sharper, harder, etched with the lines of exhaustion and a weariness that went beyond physical fatigue. It was the face of a man who had clawed his way to the top, leaving a trail of sacrifices and compromises in his wake. And the most significant sacrifice? Sakshi.

The memory of her, a vibrant splash of color in the monochrome landscape of his ambition, stabbed him with a fresh wave of regret. He thought of her laughter, the way her eyes crinkled at the corners when she smiled, the warmth of her hand in his. Those memories were buried under layers of relentless touring, grueling rehearsals, and the suffocating pressure of maintaining his carefully constructed image. He'd traded intimacy for applause, genuine connection for fleeting adoration.

He closed his eyes, the phantom touch of her lips lingering on his memory. The music, the roar of the crowds, the flashing lights – they all faded into a dull hum. He was left with the stark reality of his choices. He had become the best singer in the world, as he'd always dreamed, but at what cost? The emptiness gnawed at him, a constant, unsettling presence. He'd built a gilded cage around himself, and now he was trapped within its shimmering bars.

A sharp rap on the door jolted him from his reverie. He opened it to find Rohan, his manager, his face etched with a mixture of concern and weariness. Rohan had been with him since the beginning, a silent observer of his relentless climb to the top. He was more than a manager; he was a friend, a confidante, a witness to both his triumphs and his failures.

"Dhruva, we need to talk," Rohan said, his voice low and serious, the usual jovial tone absent. He stepped inside, his eyes scanning the opulent apartment with a mixture of awe and disapproval. The luxurious surroundings seemed to accentuate the palpable tension hanging in the air.

"What is it?" Dhruva asked, his voice raspy from disuse.

Rohan hesitated, choosing his words carefully. "The article... the one about Sakshi. It's gone viral."

Dhruva felt a chill crawl down his spine. He knew what Rohan was talking about. A gossip magazine had published an article detailing his past relationship with Sakshi, weaving a fabricated narrative of betrayal and heartbreak. It painted Sakshi as a scorned lover, using carefully chosen words and strategically leaked photos to create a scandalous narrative that threatened to derail his career. It was a calculated attack, designed to tarnish his image and destroy his meticulously built reputation.

"Who did this?" Dhruva's voice was a tight whisper, laced with a simmering rage that he hadn't felt since his schoolyard days.

Rohan shrugged, avoiding his gaze. "It's hard to say for certain. But there are whispers... suggestions that it might be someone close to you. Someone who feels... wronged."

The implication hung heavy in the air, unspoken yet deafening. Dhruva's mind raced, sifting through the faces of those closest to him: Rohan himself, his bandmates, his former friends. He couldn't fathom who would betray him so viciously, who would strike such a cowardly blow.

The weight of suspicion pressed down on him, heavy and suffocating. He realized then that his success had not only distanced him from Sakshi; it had also fractured the trust he once held dear. The glittering facade of his fame was crumbling, revealing the fissures in his carefully constructed world. He was alone, surrounded by the opulent trappings of success yet utterly desolate.

The following days were a blur of crisis meetings, damage control strategies, and frantic attempts to quell the media frenzy. His carefully curated image was shredded, replaced by a narrative he hadn't written, a story filled with betrayal and deceit. His world was collapsing, and he was powerless to stop it.

One evening, amidst the chaos, he received a cryptic email. It contained only a single photograph – a picture of him and Sakshi, taken years ago, during a quiet moment before the whirlwind of his career began. He recognized the location instantly – a small park near his old college, a place where they had shared their first hesitant kisses, their first whispered dreams.

Beneath the photograph, a single sentence: "Some things are worth more than fame."

The message was unnerving. It was a silent challenge, a taunt. He felt a surge of adrenaline, a wave of determination to uncover the truth behind the attack on his reputation and Sakshi's well-being. The calculated betrayal cut deeper than the professional damage; it threatened the very core of who he was. He realized that he couldn't simply fix the image; he had to fix himself. He needed to confront not just the betrayer but the person he had become in the pursuit of his ambitions. The confrontation wasn't just with those who had hurt him, but with his past self, the boy who had hidden his rage, the young man who had sacrificed everything for a dream that felt increasingly hollow. The crossroads of his heart led to a path far more dangerous and uncertain than any stage he'd ever graced. The path to reclaiming himself.

The Choice Between Worlds

The roar of the crowd, usually a drug, a vibrant elixir fueling his performances, felt muted tonight. The applause was a distant echo, the flashing lights a blurry haze. He stood backstage, the heavy velvet curtain a flimsy barrier between him and the thousands of faces he'd once effortlessly captivated. Now, those faces felt like a judgmental jury, their silent scrutiny weighing heavier than any critic's review. Sakshi's face flashed in his mind – her eyes, usually bright and full of life, now haunted with a fear that mirrored his own.

The anonymous message – a chilling digital whisper – had struck at the heart of everything. It hadn't just threatened his carefully constructed career; it had threatened Sakshi, the one constant in a life that felt increasingly unsteady. The accusations were ludicrous, fabricated, designed to dismantle him professionally and emotionally. But the precision of the attack, the knowledge it displayed of his most private moments, suggested an insider, someone close, someone he trusted.

His manager, Mark, a shrewd, pragmatic man who'd guided his career with a steely focus, stood beside him, his usually confident demeanor laced with a rare apprehension. "Dhruva," Mark began, his voice low, "We need to act. The press is swarming. We can spin this, control the narrative, but..." He trailed off, his gaze conveying the unspoken truth: damage control only went so far. The seed of doubt had been planted, and it was taking root in fertile ground.

Dhruva's gut twisted. He felt the cold knot of fear tightening in his chest. He'd built this empire, brick by painstaking brick, each note, each performance a testament to years of relentless dedication. It was a fragile edifice, and now, a single, malicious blow threatened to crumble it all. But the threat to Sakshi was far more devastating. The thought of her, vulnerable and alone, facing this storm, was a visceral blow. He felt a familiar, simmering rage, the same rage he'd buried as a boy, now threatening to erupt.

His phone buzzed. It was a call from a number he didn't recognize. He hesitated, a flicker of apprehension dancing in his gut. He could ignore it, bury himself in the denials and carefully constructed statements, play the game of public relations, but a deeper instinct, a primal urge to confront the darkness, urged him to answer.

The voice on the other end was calm, almost chillingly so. It was a voice laced with a hint of familiarity, but he couldn't quite place it. The voice laid out further details of the attack, details that confirmed the insidiousness of the plot. It was a well-orchestrated campaign, designed not just to discredit him, but to destroy him.

The voice offered a solution, a way to halt the bleeding, to silence the accusers. It involved a specific course of action, a quid pro quo, a trade-off that sent a shiver down his spine. It was a devil's bargain, a choice between the carefully constructed image, his glittering career, and a chance to protect Sakshi, to unravel the truth behind the brutal attack.

He hung up, the cold New York air suddenly feeling heavier, the silence amplified in his ears. The choice was laid bare, stark and unforgiving. He could fight back, engage in a public war, a messy, brutal battle that could consume him entirely, leaving him wounded and possibly defeated. He could pour all his resources, his energy, his emotional reserves into protecting his career, battling the lies, proving his innocence. But that would leave Sakshi exposed, vulnerable to the venomous whispers. And even if he won the battle, the war would have left scars, deep and enduring.

Alternatively, he could take the risk, a path far more treacherous and uncertain. The voice on the phone had proposed a deal that would undoubtedly tarnish his image, raise questions, and maybe even land him in deep legal trouble. But it was the only way, perhaps, to protect Sakshi and unravel the plot against them. The choice felt like navigating a minefield blindfolded, each step carrying the potential for catastrophic consequences.

The weight of the world pressed down on him. The years of hard work, the sacrifices, the relentless pursuit of his dreams —all of it felt insignificant, reduced to mere pawns in a larger, more sinister game. His carefully constructed world, the one he had labored so hard to build, was crumbling around him. The pressure mounted, the silence amplifying his internal turmoil.

He paced the backstage area, his thoughts a chaotic storm. He had always been a man of control, a meticulous planner, yet this crisis felt beyond his reach, beyond the scope of his carefully crafted strategies. The accusations, while absurd, held a chilling resonance of truth, exploiting weaknesses, insecurities, vulnerabilities he had never fully addressed. It was as if his entire life, meticulously curated and crafted, was being dissected and laid bare for public consumption.

The thought of Sakshi again filled his mind. Her face, etched with worry and fear, was a haunting image. The choice wasn't just about his career; it was about her safety, her peace of mind. It was a choice between two worlds – the glittering world of fame and fortune he'd painstakingly built, and a darker, more uncertain path that held the potential for both destruction and redemption.

He thought of his journey, the years spent honing his craft, enduring ridicule and hardship, climbing the ladder rung by rung until he had reached the pinnacle of his profession. The sacrifices he'd made – the missed birthdays, the neglected friendships, the emotional toll of relentless touring and public scrutiny – all seemed inconsequential now, overshadowed by the magnitude of this crisis.

His ambition, once a burning fire, now felt like a hollow shell, a relentless pursuit that had ultimately led him to this precipice. He wondered if the cost had been worth it, if the price of his success was too high, if the hollow accolades were a worthy trade for the happiness and peace he craved. The choice before him was not just a professional one; it was a deeply personal and moral reckoning, forcing him to confront the very essence of who he was, what he valued, and what he was willing to sacrifice.

He pictured the faces of his loyal fans, their unwavering support the bedrock of his success. The thought of betraying their trust, of letting them down, felt like a gut punch. But could he justify preserving his image, protecting his reputation, at the cost of Sakshi's well-being? The scales felt weighted, heavily tipped towards a sacrifice he wasn't sure he could bear.

Hours bled into each other, the tension in the room thicker than the pre-show jitters he was used to. Mark's occasional glances were filled with unspoken concern, his silence more telling than any words could have been. The silence of the backstage area was only broken by the distant echoes of the concert that was going on, a cruel irony given the turmoil raging inside him.

The choice hung heavy in the air, a suffocating pressure that threatened to crush him. It was a crossroads, a turning point, a moment that would define not just his career, but the trajectory of his life. He knew, with a chilling certainty, that this decision would irrevocably alter the course of his future, shaping him in ways he couldn't fully comprehend. And as the weight of the decision pressed down upon him, he realized he was not just choosing between two worlds, but between two versions of himself – the ambitious, successful singer and the man willing to sacrifice everything for the woman he loved. The choice was his, and the consequences would be far-reaching. The silence was broken only by the rhythmic beating of his own heart, a drumbeat of uncertainty echoing the crossroads of his soul. The stakes were high, and the path forward remained shrouded in darkness.

Risky Gambit

The backstage air hung thick with the scent of sweat, stale perfume, and nervous anticipation. The muffled roar of the crowd felt like a distant thunderstorm, its power diluted by the oppressive weight of his decision. He paced, the polished floor cold beneath his bare feet, the rhythmic squeak a counterpoint to the frantic beat of his heart. He'd spent hours agonizing over this, dissecting every possible outcome, every potential consequence, until his mind felt frayed and exhausted. He'd built this empire, brick by painstaking brick, note by perfectly executed note. His career was a skyscraper scraping the heavens, a testament to years of relentless dedication, sacrifice, and sheer willpower. And now, he was about to risk it all on a single, desperate gamble.

He glanced at his reflection in the darkened mirror. The face staring back was pale, etched with exhaustion and a profound uncertainty. The carefully crafted persona, the confident superstar, had crumbled, leaving behind a vulnerable young man wrestling with a love that threatened to consume him. He ran a hand through his hair, the gesture revealing a tremor he hadn't realized he possessed. He was no longer the master of his own fate, but a puppet dancing to the tune of his heart. And that heart was beating a frantic rhythm, a drum solo of fear and hope intertwined.

His manager, Mr. Sharma, a man known for his icy demeanor and unwavering pragmatism, had warned him repeatedly. "Dhruva," he'd said, his voice a low growl, "This Sakshi... she's a distraction. A liability. You're on the precipice of something truly monumental. Don't jeopardize it all for a fleeting romance." But Mr. Sharma didn't understand. He couldn't grasp the depth of the chasm that separated him from the world of fame and fortune, and the simple, unadulterated joy he found in Sakshi's presence.

The risk was monumental. A public display of affection, a blatant disregard for the carefully constructed image of the enigmatic, unattainable superstar, could shatter his carefully curated persona. The tabloids would feast, the fans would turn, and sponsors would vanish like wisps of smoke. His career, the culmination of a lifetime's ambition, could crumble into dust. The chilling possibility sent a wave of nausea through him, the metallic tang of fear coating his tongue.

Yet, the thought of losing Sakshi, of letting her slip away like sand through his fingers, was unbearable. He remembered the way her laughter used to fill his small apartment, the way her eyes held a universe of unspoken emotions, the way her touch could calm the storm raging within him. Those memories were more precious than any award, any accolade, any amount of fame. They were the bedrock of his happiness, the foundation upon which he'd built his life. And now, those memories felt like fragile shards of glass, threatening to shatter at any moment.

He took a deep breath, trying to steady his nerves, his hands still trembling slightly. He had a plan, a reckless, audacious plan, born of desperation and fueled by a desperate hope. It was a gamble, a risky, all-or-nothing bet on a love that might be nothing more than a beautiful illusion. But he was willing to roll the dice. He owed it to himself, to Sakshi, and to that small, quiet boy who had once dreamed of a life beyond the confines of his quiet existence.

He glanced at his watch. The time was approaching. He smoothed down his shirt, took one last look in the mirror, and steeled his resolve. He would walk out on that stage, not as the polished, unapproachable superstar, but as Dhruva, a young man risking everything for the woman he loved. The roar of the crowd was deafening now, almost a physical force pushing against him. But this time, he wasn't afraid. He was armed with a weapon far more potent than any microphone or guitar – a desperate, unwavering love.

He walked out onto the stage, the spotlight blinding, the expectant hush of the audience palpable. He saw Sakshi, nestled among the crowd, her eyes filled with a mixture of anticipation and apprehension. He smiled, a genuine, unguarded smile that reached his eyes. He started to sing, his voice a raw, emotional outpouring that resonated with the truth of his feelings. He didn't stick to the pre-arranged setlist. Instead, he sang a song he'd written for Sakshi, a ballad of quiet longing and unyielding devotion.

The lyrics poured from his heart, each note carrying the weight of his emotions, the vulnerability of his gamble. He sang about the sacrifices he had made, about the dreams he'd chased, about the constant struggle between ambition and love. The lyrics weren't sugar-coated or poetic, they were raw, honest, and painfully real. He confessed his fears, his insecurities, and the desperate hope that flickered within his heart. As he sang, his eyes locked with Sakshi's, and he poured every ounce of his love into the performance.

The crowd fell silent, captivated by the raw emotion, the palpable vulnerability. His voice filled the vast arena, each note echoing the tumultuous journey of his heart. He was no longer a polished performer, but a man baring his soul to the world. He sang about the fear of failure, the weight of expectation, and the intoxicating allure of a love that threatened to upend everything he had worked for. He sang of the constant battle between his ambition and his heart, a battle that had raged within him for years.

The song ended, the silence lingering, heavy with unspoken emotions. The expected applause was slow to start, hesitant, almost respectful. Then, it began, a wave of sound that crashed over him, a torrent of appreciation for the courage he'd displayed, for the truth he'd revealed. The silence was broken by a thunderous applause, a wave of emotion washing over the audience. It wasn't the usual, adoring applause, but something deeper, more profound. It was applause mixed with understanding, acceptance, and a sense of shared vulnerability. They had witnessed not just a performance, but a confession, a raw and honest exposition of a young man's soul.

As he stepped off the stage, he saw Sakshi waiting for him, her eyes shining with tears. He didn't know what the future held, what the consequences of his risky gamble would be. His career might be in jeopardy, his carefully constructed image might lie in ruins. But as he embraced Sakshi, as he felt her arms around him, he knew, with a certainty that transcended any fear, that he had made the right choice. He had risked everything for love, and in that moment, he felt a peace he had never known before. The future remained uncertain, but he wasn't afraid anymore. He had faced his crossroads and chosen the path of his heart. And in that choice, he found a strength, a resilience, he never knew he possessed. The risk had been monumental, the gamble audacious, but in the end, the reward was immeasurable. The love he had found, the honesty he'd embraced, had given his life a meaning beyond the glittering facade of his success. He had chosen love, and that, he knew, was a victory far greater than any he had ever achieved on stage.

The days that followed were a whirlwind of anticipation and apprehension. The headlines screamed, the gossip columns buzzed, and the speculation ran rampant. Some lauded his bravery, others condemned his recklessness. His manager, Mr. Sharma, remained tight-lipped, his silence a testament to the storm raging within him. The sponsors were hesitant, their decisions hanging in the balance.

But amidst the chaos, Dhruva found solace in Sakshi's arms. They spent hours talking, sharing their fears, their hopes, and their dreams. He knew that their future was uncertain, that the path ahead would be fraught with challenges, but he was no longer afraid. He had found something far more valuable than fame or fortune: a love that was strong enough to weather any storm. He had gambled his career, his reputation, his entire future on a single, desperate act of love. And, despite the uncertainty, he knew, deep down, that it was the best gamble he had ever made. He had chosen authenticity over artifice, love over ambition, and in that choice, he had found himself.

Unexpected Betrayal

The adrenaline rush of the sold-out concert faded, replaced by a chilling emptiness. The roar of the crowd, once a comforting wave, now felt like a distant echo, mocking the quiet dread that settled in Dhruva's chest. He'd chosen love, risked everything for Sakshi, and the initial euphoria of that decision was slowly curdling into something far more sinister. He'd thought he'd faced the biggest challenges already, navigating the treacherous waters of the music industry, silencing the doubts that gnawed at his soul, and battling his own insecurities. He'd conquered those demons, emerging victorious, yet a new, insidious enemy had emerged from the shadows – betrayal.

It started subtly, a misplaced file, a missed phone call, a whispered conversation overheard in the corridor of his recording studio. Initially, Dhruva dismissed these incidents as mere coincidences, the inevitable glitches in the complex machinery of his life. He was, after all, surrounded by people: managers, agents, publicists, assistants – a sprawling network of individuals all with their own agendas. But the irregularities multiplied, becoming harder to ignore, harder to dismiss as mere coincidence. His meticulously planned tour schedule began to unravel, bookings mysteriously cancelled, vital contracts vanishing into thin air. His financial advisor reported discrepancies in his accounts, losses he couldn't explain. The whispers intensified, morphing from speculation into accusations, from rumours into hard, cold facts.

The betrayal came from Rohan, his closest confidante, his right-hand man, the one person he'd trusted implicitly. Rohan, who had been with him since the beginning, who had shared his dreams, his struggles, his triumphs. Rohan, who had seen him at his lowest and his highest, who had known the depths of his vulnerability. The irony was a cruel, sharp blade twisting in Dhruva's gut.

The revelation hit him like a physical blow. He found Rohan, not in his office, but in a clandestine meeting with a rival record label executive, documents scattered across the table – documents Dhruva recognized instantly as confidential contracts, his own contracts, altered, signed, ready to be finalized. Rohan's face, usually bright and jovial, was a mask of cold calculation. The betrayal wasn't just a professional slight; it was a deep, personal wound. It was a violation of trust so profound it threatened to shatter Dhruva's carefully constructed world.

The ensuing confrontation was brutal. Words, sharp and accusatory, flew between them, a silent battle fought amidst the hushed tones of the office. Rohan didn't deny it. His justification, laced with bitterness and resentment, was a twisted narrative of Dhruva's success overshadowing his own. He claimed he was simply seizing his opportunity, a chance to escape Dhruva's colossal shadow, to finally step into the limelight himself. He painted himself as a victim, a loyal friend betrayed by ambition, a pawn in a larger game of power and greed. It was a chillingly convincing performance, delivered with the cold precision of a seasoned actor. But the truth lay in the betrayal itself, a stark, undeniable act that had ripped apart years of friendship and loyalty.

The legal battles that followed were relentless, draining, a grueling marathon through the muddied waters of corporate law. Dhruva, accustomed to the spotlight, found himself battling in the shadows, fighting not just for his career but for his very sense of self. The image he had painstakingly crafted – the talented singer, the sensitive artist, the humble success story – was now under attack, smeared by accusations and counter-accusations. The media frenzy was deafening, a whirlwind of speculation and conjecture, his name splashed across headlines, dissected and debated, his reputation hanging precariously in the balance.

He lost a significant portion of his assets, deals were cancelled, and his once-solid reputation was tarnished. He found himself isolated, abandoned by those who had once flocked around him, their loyalty evaporating like morning mist. The world he'd built, painstakingly crafted from years of sacrifice and hard work, crumbled around him, revealing the harsh, unforgiving nature of the industry he'd conquered.

But amidst the chaos and despair, Dhruva discovered a strength he hadn't known he possessed. He found solace in Sakshi's unwavering support, her love a beacon in the storm. He faced the legal battles with a grim determination, refusing to be broken. He channeled his grief and anger into his music, his voice pouring forth emotions so raw and powerful they moved his audiences to tears. His music became his weapon, his testimony, a testament to his resilience.

He had faced setbacks before, moments when his dreams felt out of reach, when self-doubt threatened to engulf him. But this was different. This wasn't a momentary dip; this was a catastrophic fall. He felt the weight of his loss, the hollowness of his betrayal, but it was this very loss that fuelled his determination to fight back. He knew that his fight was not just for his career, for his fortune, but for his soul. It was a fight for his integrity, for his identity, for the man he had become and the man he aspired to be.

His legal team worked tirelessly, sifting through mountains of documents, uncovering evidence of Rohan's fraudulent activities. They unearthed a complex web of deceit, revealing a conspiracy that extended far beyond Rohan, implicating other individuals within the music industry. It was a systematic dismantling of Dhruva's empire, orchestrated with ruthless precision and icy calculation. The revelation sent shockwaves through the industry, exposing the dark underbelly of fame and fortune, the cutthroat competition, the ruthless pursuit of power.

The trial became a public spectacle, a battle played out under the harsh glare of the media spotlight. The courtroom transformed into an arena, where Dhruva faced his betrayer, their clash a visceral battle of wills, a duel fought with words, with evidence, with truth. The weight of the accusations, the public scrutiny, the emotional toll – it tested him to his limits. He endured sleepless nights, his mind racing, replaying every detail, analyzing every possibility. He stood before the court not just as a celebrated singer, but as a victim, a man who had been betrayed by someone he considered a brother.

In the end, justice prevailed. Rohan and his accomplices were exposed, their actions laid bare for all to see. Though he lost much, Dhruva's name was cleared, his integrity restored. The victory was bittersweet, the price steep, but he emerged stronger, his spirit unbent, his resolve hardened. He had faced the darkness and emerged into the light, a testament to his strength, his resilience, his unwavering faith in himself. The experience reshaped him, deepened his understanding of human nature, the complexities of relationships, and the fickle nature of trust. He understood that the journey to success was a lonely one, paved with sacrifices and betrayals, that even at the peak of his achievements, he was not immune to the harsh realities of life. He had lost much, but he had gained something far more valuable: a profound understanding of himself, his strengths, and his vulnerabilities. He emerged not just as the greatest singer in the world, but a survivor, a warrior who had faced the darkness and emerged victorious, bearing the scars of his battles as badges of honour.

A Shattered Dream

The champagne tasted like ash in Dhruva's mouth. The celebratory after-party, a whirlwind of flashing cameras and sycophantic smiles, felt like a grotesque parody of joy. He forced a smile, a rictus of strained amusement plastered onto his face, as he accepted another congratulatory handshake. The whispers followed him like shadows – whispers of his meteoric rise, his unparalleled talent, his untouchable success. But the accolades felt hollow, the applause a distant rumble, drowned out by the deafening silence in his heart.

Sakshi. The name was a phantom limb, a constant ache in his soul. He'd risked everything for her, jeopardized his career, his reputation, his very sanity, only to have her vanish without a trace. The meticulously crafted façade of his carefully constructed life was crumbling around him, brick by agonizing brick. The betrayal stung more than the physical wounds he'd sustained during the ordeal with Rohan; it was a betrayal that carved a deeper, more permanent scar on his soul.

The initial euphoria of exposing Rohan's treachery, the sweet taste of justice, had quickly turned sour. The legal battles, the media frenzy, the relentless scrutiny, it had all taken its toll. He had won, yes, but the victory tasted like defeat. The price of his triumph was too high. He'd lost not only Sakshi, but also the innocence he once possessed, the unwavering belief in the inherent goodness of people. The world he had known, the world he had meticulously built, had shattered into a million fragments.

His phone buzzed, the vibration a jarring intrusion into his numb state. He looked down, his breath catching in his throat. The name on the screen sent a jolt of icy fear through him. It was an unknown number, but the text message was chillingly succinct: "You can't hide forever, Dhruva. We know what you did."

Panic clawed at his throat. He felt a primal fear, a terror that transcended the rational, that dug its claws into his very being. The words echoed in his mind, a sinister mantra, whispering of hidden truths and impending doom. Who was this? What did they know? The meticulous plan he'd developed to get his life back on track after the trauma he had endured seemed to collapse under the weight of this unknown threat.

He tried to rationalize it, to dismiss it as a prank, a misguided attempt at intimidation. But a deep-seated unease gnawed at him, a feeling that something far more sinister was at play. The shadowy figure from his past, the one he thought he'd vanquished, seemed to be re-emerging from the darkness, stronger and more menacing than ever before.

The following days were a blur of paranoia and sleepless nights. He hired a security detail, a team of stoic professionals who moved around him like silent sentinels. Their presence was a constant reminder of the danger that lurked, the unseen enemy who held him in their sights. He lived a life of constant vigilance, scanning every face, every shadow, every whisper. He avoided public appearances, canceling concerts and interviews, retreating into a self-imposed exile. His meticulously crafted public image, the persona he had spent years cultivating, began to disintegrate under the unrelenting pressure.

His manager, Arjun, was frantic. His pleas for Dhruva to resume his career fell on deaf ears. The once-vibrant, charismatic singer was replaced by a hollow shell, haunted by fear and consumed by paranoia. The phone continued to buzz with cryptic messages, each one chipping away at his sanity, each one reinforcing the terrifying certainty that he was not alone in his struggle. That someone, or something, was watching him, waiting for the opportune moment to strike.

He sought solace in his music, pouring his fear and anguish into his melodies. His songs, once vibrant and full of life, now resonated with a chilling undercurrent of despair. They became a diary of his descent into darkness, a raw and unflinching portrait of a man battling his inner demons and the very real threat looming over him.

One evening, huddled in his secluded recording studio, the phone rang. He hesitated, his hand trembling as he reached for the receiver. He knew, deep down, that he couldn't ignore it. He couldn't continue to run.

"Dhruva," a voice whispered, a voice he recognized, a voice that sent a cold shiver down his spine. It was Sakshi. Her voice, once a beacon of light and hope, was now laced with a chilling undertone, a sinister edge that spoke of betrayal and deceit.

"Sakshi? Is that really you?" he whispered, his voice barely audible.

"It's me, Dhruva," she said, her voice dripping with a cold venom he never thought possible. "And I have so much to tell you."

The conversation was a slow drip of poison. Sakshi revealed her involvement with Rohan, not as a victim, but as a willing accomplice, a partner in his scheme to sabotage Dhruva's career. She spoke of resentment, of jealousy, of a burning desire for revenge for something that Dhruva had inadvertently done long ago. A past Dhruva couldn't recall. A past he now had to confront.

Her words were a blow to his already shattered psyche, shattering the last vestiges of his hope. The betrayal was absolute, complete, devastating. It wasn't just Rohan's treachery; it was the betrayal of the woman he loved, the woman he'd sacrificed everything for.

The call ended abruptly, leaving Dhruva alone in the darkness, the weight of the revelation pressing down on him with crushing force. He had survived Rohan's machinations, emerged victorious from the legal battle, but this, this was a different kind of warfare. A war of hearts, a war waged in the shadows, a war where he was fighting not just for his life, his career, but for his very soul.

The chilling realization washed over him: he had underestimated his enemies. He had underestimated the depths of human depravity. He had underestimated the lengths to which someone would go to exact revenge.

He looked out of the studio window, the city lights twinkling below, a stark contrast to the darkness that had enveloped him. His dreams, once so vibrant, so full of promise, were now shattered fragments scattered across the floor of his life. His career, his reputation, his love, it had all crumbled like a poorly constructed house of cards.

His journey had taken him to the pinnacle of success, but now, he found himself standing at a crossroads, facing an abyss of unimaginable darkness. He had conquered the challenges of the music industry, the treacherous waters of fame, but this new battle, this war against the shadows of his past, was a fight for survival. A fight he might not survive.

The question now was not whether he would reach the peak of his career again, but whether he would even survive to see another sunrise. The answer, as he looked out into the night, remained elusive, shrouded in the same darkness that had consumed his shattered dreams.

Facing the Aftermath

The world, once a vibrant stage for his triumphant performances, now felt like a suffocating cage. The applause, once a roaring wave that lifted him to euphoric heights, was replaced by a deafening silence – a silence that echoed the emptiness in his soul. The betrayal, sharp and brutal, had cleaved through the carefully constructed facade of his success, leaving him exposed and vulnerable. The glittering awards, symbols of his hard-won achievements, now seemed like mocking reminders of his naiveté. He had climbed to the pinnacle of his ambition, only to find himself standing alone on a precipice, the wind of his own making whipping around him, threatening to topple him into the abyss.

The aftermath of the scandal was a slow, agonizing descent. The headlines screamed of his downfall, twisting his story into a sensationalized caricature. His name, once synonymous with musical genius, became a byword for betrayal and deception. The once-adoring fans, their faces blurred behind the frenzy of flashing cameras, now hurled accusations and insults. The weight of their disappointment, their anger, pressed down on him, suffocating him with its intensity. His carefully curated image, crafted with years of meticulous effort, crumbled to dust, replaced by the raw, unfiltered reality of his mistakes. He was no longer the untouchable superstar; he was just Dhruva, a young man grappling with the shattering consequences of his choices.

His meticulously designed life had imploded, taking with it not only his career but also his sense of self. He had sacrificed so much – relationships, time, even a part of himself – to achieve his dream. And now, in the cold light of day, the sacrifice felt meaningless, a bitter testament to the transient nature of fame and fortune. The opulent mansion, once a symbol of his success, now felt like a gilded cage, its walls closing in on him, magnifying his isolation. His days were spent in a haze of self-recrimination, each moment a cruel reminder of the choices that had led him to this desolate place.

Sleep offered no escape. Nightmares plagued him, their shadowy tendrils wrapping around him, replaying the betrayal, the accusations, the crushing weight of disappointment. He would wake up in a cold sweat, the remnants of the nightmare clinging to him like a shroud. The silence of the empty rooms pressed in on him, amplifying the echoes of his own self-doubt. Even the music, his solace, his refuge, had turned against him, each note a painful reminder of the world he had lost. The melodies he had once poured his soul into now felt hollow, devoid of the passion and joy they once held.

The days bled into one another, each indistinguishable from the last, marked only by the steady drip, drip, drip of his despair. He tried to find solace in simple things – a quiet walk in the park, a solitary cup of tea, the distant murmur of the city that once celebrated him. But even these small comforts felt tainted, their sweetness overshadowed by the bitterness of his situation. He was adrift, lost in a sea of his own making, with no compass to guide him, no shore to steer towards. The world had turned its back, and he had no one to turn to. The silence, once a refuge, now felt like a condemnation, a constant reminder of his fall from grace.

His agent, once his staunch advocate, now avoided his calls. His record label, once eager to promote him, issued carefully worded press releases emphasizing a need for "personal time." His once-vibrant social media feeds remained stubbornly silent – a stark contrast to the tempest of negativity that raged in the outside world. The only person who reached out was Sakshi, her voice a fragile thread of hope in the vast emptiness of his life. But even her support couldn't fully penetrate the thick fog of his despair. The weight of his actions, the depth of his betrayal, felt insurmountable. He had hurt too many people, damaged too many lives, to ever truly expect forgiveness.

The confrontation, when it came, was not the dramatic showdown he had perhaps anticipated. There were no fiery speeches, no grand pronouncements of justice. It was a quiet meeting, held in the hushed sanctity of a small, dimly lit room. The person responsible for his downfall, a former friend, sat across from him, their face pale and drawn, their eyes filled with a mixture of guilt and regret. There was no outburst of anger, no accusations traded. Just a heavy, uncomfortable silence broken only by the occasional nervous cough. Dhruva saw the hurt in his friend's eyes, the burden of their actions weighing heavily upon them. It was a silent acknowledgment of their shared guilt. The revelation that followed, the slow unraveling of the truth, was less a shocking twist and more a gradual sinking into a deeper, darker understanding of the complexities that drove their actions. It was a recognition that mistakes could have cascading, devastating consequences, a reality they were forced to face together.

The silence that followed the confrontation was different. It wasn't the deafening silence of his downfall, the silence of judgment and condemnation. This was a quiet acceptance, a shared understanding of the irrevocable damage done. It was a silence pregnant with the unspoken weight of loss, regret, and the painful process of healing. In that silence, Dhruva began to find a fragile kind of peace. The peace of acceptance, however painful. The realization that forgiveness, if it ever came, was a long and arduous journey, not a simple resolution.

The road to recovery was long and arduous, filled with moments of doubt and despair. But amidst the wreckage of his shattered life, Dhruva began to rebuild, one painstaking brick at a time. He sought professional help, confronting the demons that had haunted him for so long. He spent time with family, allowing himself to be vulnerable, to lean on those who loved him unconditionally. The support he received was a slow but steady balm to his wounds. Slowly, painstakingly, he began to piece himself back together. He rediscovered his passion for music, finding solace in the creative process, channeling his pain and self-loathing into new melodies, new rhythms. He found purpose not in fame or fortune, but in the art itself.

The weight of silence, once his tormentor, became his ally. In the quiet solitude, he learned to listen to the inner voice that had been drowned out by the noise of his success. He discovered a strength he never knew he possessed. The process of healing wasn't about erasing the past but about integrating it into his story, acknowledging the mistakes while also embracing the lessons learned. He learned to forgive himself, not for the sake of others, but for his own sanity. The scars remained, visible reminders of his fall from grace, but they were also badges of honor, symbols of his resilience, of his capacity to overcome the depths of despair.

He never regained the dizzying heights of his previous fame, but he discovered a different kind of fulfillment, a quiet joy that was less about public acclaim and more about personal integrity. He discovered that true success wasn't about reaching the top of the mountain, but about the strength and compassion that emerged from the struggle to climb back up after a devastating fall. The echoes of silence, once a symphony of despair, gradually faded into a hum of hope, a gentle reminder that even in the deepest darkness, there is always the possibility of a new beginning. And as he stood on the threshold of this new beginning, he looked forward not with ambition but with a gentle sense of acceptance, a profound understanding of the intricate dance between success and failure, and a quiet confidence in his ability to navigate the unknown paths that lay ahead.

A Reckoning

The rain lashed against the panoramic windows of his penthouse apartment, mirroring the tempest raging inside him. He hadn't seen Rohan in years, not since the meticulously planned smear campaign had shattered his career, leaving him a pariah in the industry he'd once ruled. Rohan, his former manager, the man who'd promised him the world, then systematically ripped it away. Tonight, that would change.

The heavy oak door creaked open, revealing Rohan, looking older, wearier, the sharp edges of his ambition dulled by the passage of time. He hadn't anticipated Dhruva's invitation. The unspoken accusation hung heavy in the air, thicker than the scent of expensive cologne Rohan tried to mask his nervousness with.

"Dhruva," Rohan began, his voice a strained whisper, "I... I didn't expect this."

Dhruva didn't speak, his gaze unwavering. He gestured to the chair opposite him, the polished mahogany gleaming under the dim light. The silence stretched, taut and suffocating, punctuated only by the relentless drumming of the rain. It was a silence that felt familiar, a chilling echo of the silence that had followed the public exposure of the fabricated scandal.

Rohan sat, his hands clasped tightly in his lap, his eyes darting around the opulent room. The lavish surroundings were a stark contrast to the haunted look in his eyes. He had underestimated Dhruva then, assumed his quiet nature translated into weakness. He was wrong.

"I... I was desperate," Rohan finally mumbled, his voice barely audible. "The pressure... the competition... I thought... I thought a little nudge would secure your position."

Dhruva's lips curled into a bitter smile. "A little nudge? Rohan, you destroyed me. You built me up, only to watch me fall. You savored my demise."

Rohan flinched, the words hitting their mark. The carefully constructed facade of remorse crumbled. "It wasn't supposed to be like this. The articles... they were supposed to be damaging, yes, but not... not this devastating." He shifted uncomfortably, his eyes flickering nervously. "I just wanted more. For both of us."

"More?" Dhruva's voice was low, dangerously calm. "More money? More power? You sacrificed my integrity, my happiness, my entire life for your insatiable greed."

Rohan avoided his gaze, his fingers tracing patterns on the arm of the chair. "I... I panicked. I lost control. The deals... the contracts... everything was on the line. I believed if you fell, I could rise."

The rain intensified, the wind howling like a banshee outside. The storm mirrored the chaos within the room. Dhruva rose slowly from his chair, his shadow looming large over Rohan.

"You believed you were smarter than me. Stronger than me," Dhruva said, his voice a chilling whisper. "You thought you could manipulate me, use me, and discard me like a broken toy."

He paced before Rohan, the rhythmic sound of his footsteps adding to the tension. "You were wrong. I'm not the same quiet boy you knew. I've spent years rebuilding, not just my career, but myself. And I've learned a lot. I learned that silence can be a weapon, just as deafening as a roar."

Rohan's eyes widened with dawning fear. He tried to speak, but his voice caught in his throat. The weight of his actions, the consequences of his betrayal, finally crashed down on him.

Dhruva stopped pacing, standing directly in front of Rohan, his eyes piercing. "I could destroy you now. I could expose everything, ruin your life like you ruined mine. But that's not what I want."

Rohan looked up, a flicker of hope igniting in his eyes.

"No," Dhruva continued, his voice softening only slightly, "I want something more... satisfying. I want you to understand what you took from me. I want you to feel the pain you inflicted. The loneliness, the isolation, the crushing weight of betrayal."

He leaned in, his voice dropping to a near-whisper. "I want you to live with that. Every single day. For the rest of your life."

He turned and walked away, leaving Rohan alone in the opulent room, the rain continuing its relentless assault on the windows. The silence, this time, was not an echo of emptiness, but a chilling testament to Dhruva's power, a power he'd discovered not in the spotlight, but in the quiet strength of forgiveness. A forgiveness that was far more potent, far more devastating, than any revenge.

The next morning, Rohan woke up to find a single, unmarked envelope on his bedside table. Inside, was a meticulously compiled file detailing every aspect of his fraudulent activities. It wasn't enough to bring him down legally, but it was enough to ensure that the music industry, the industry he craved to rule, would never touch him again. The silence that followed was self-imposed, a quiet exile from the world he had so ruthlessly manipulated. His career, his reputation, his life, were effectively over. The price of his ambition, his betrayal, was far higher than he had ever imagined.

Dhruva, meanwhile, found a strange peace. He was no longer the naive young man who had been so easily manipulated. He had endured, he had rebuilt, and he had emerged stronger, wiser, and with a profound understanding of the complexities of human nature. His voice, once silenced by betrayal, now resonated with a newfound strength, a strength born from resilience and a deep-seated understanding of the consequences of unchecked ambition. He didn't return to the dizzying heights of his past fame, but he found a different kind of success, a quiet success built on integrity and the unwavering belief in his own worth. He began to write music again, composing songs that spoke of resilience, of healing, and of the quiet triumph of the human spirit.

The echoes of silence that had once haunted him, now served as a constant reminder of the lessons he'd learned, the battles he'd won, and the profound sense of self he had finally discovered. His journey wasn't over, but he approached the future with a newfound clarity, a quiet strength, and a deep understanding that true success lay not in the applause of the masses, but in the peace he found within himself. The world might have once silenced him, but he had found his own voice, a voice stronger and more resonant than ever before.

He understood now that the silence wasn't the end, but a necessary prelude to a new beginning, a new song, a new life. He had faced his demons, and in doing so, he had finally found himself. The journey had been brutal, but the melody of his life, once shattered, was slowly, beautifully, rebuilding itself. His heart, once wounded, was beginning to sing again. A new song was taking shape, a melody of resilience, a symphony of self-discovery. The silence was finally broken.

Acceptance and Loss

The city lights, a million shimmering pinpricks against the inky canvas of the night, held no allure. He sat on his balcony, the cool night air a stark contrast to the fire that still flickered within him, a low ember of resentment and regret. The rain had stopped, leaving behind a glistening cityscape, a deceptive sheen of peace. Inside, the penthouse apartment was opulent, a testament to his success, yet it felt hollow, a gilded cage echoing with the ghosts of what could have been. He thought of Sakshi, her face a vivid memory, sharp and clear even after all these years. The ache in his chest was a familiar companion, a constant reminder of the sacrifices he'd made, the choices he'd been forced to make.

His music career had reached unimaginable heights. Stadiums roared with his name, critics lauded his talent, and awards lined his shelves like trophies in a macabre game. Yet, the applause felt muted, distant, like echoes in an empty cathedral. The victory tasted like ash. He had conquered the world, but the battle within remained unresolved, a silent war waged in the quiet corners of his heart.

He recalled the night Rohan had betrayed him, the calculated cruelty of the smear campaign, the vicious whispers that had attempted to silence him. It had been a brutal fight for survival, a desperate scramble to reclaim his name, his integrity, his very self. He'd emerged victorious, but the scars remained, etched deep into his soul. The victory had come at a price – a price he wasn't entirely sure he was willing to pay. The emptiness he felt wasn't a void, but a cavernous space filled with the ghosts of missed opportunities, of paths not taken, of a love that had slipped through his fingers like grains of sand.

The phone buzzed, a jarring interruption to his somber reverie. He glanced at the screen – it was Anya, his publicist. He sighed, a weary exhale that carried the weight of years. He knew what she wanted – another interview, another promotional event, another conquest in the relentless pursuit of maintaining his celebrity status. He felt a surge of irritation, a prickle of rebellion against the machine that had propelled him to success, yet simultaneously trapped him within its gilded cage.

He silenced his phone, the vibration still resonating against his palm, a microcosm of the discord within him. He thought of his parents, their unwavering support throughout his tumultuous journey, their pride a constant source of strength. He owed them everything, and the thought of disappointing them, of letting them down after all they'd sacrificed, was a burden he couldn't bear. Yet, the pursuit of this elusive success had cost him something immeasurable, something he couldn't quantify, or even fully understand. He had climbed the ladder, but he had done so alone, leaving behind the most precious things along the way.

He stood up, the cool night air a welcome slap against his skin. He walked to the window, looking out at the sprawling city, a tapestry of light and shadow, a mirror reflecting his own internal turmoil. The acceptance he craved wasn't a simple switch he could flip. It was a slow, agonizing process of confronting his demons, acknowledging his losses, and learning to live with the echoes of what had been.

He had won the battle, but he had lost the war. Or had he? He looked down at the city stretching before him, each light a tiny life, each struggle a silent testament to the complexities of existence. He was not alone in his pain, his struggle, his triumphs. The world, for all its harsh realities, for all its betrayals and disappointments, was full of stories, full of experiences, both joyous and tragic, and it was within the embrace of that shared humanity that he might find the peace he sought.

He picked up his phone, hesitating for a moment before answering Anya's call. He wouldn't let the emptiness consume him. He would continue to sing, to create, to share his music with the world. But this time, it would be different. His music would not just be a reflection of his ambition, but also of his vulnerabilities, his losses, his resilience. He would sing not just for the applause, but for himself, for the healing power of creation, for the quiet moments of acceptance that he had begun to discover.

The loss of Sakshi, the betrayal of Rohan, the relentless pressure of the industry – these were not just events in his past, but chapters in a life that was still being written. He had learned to navigate the darkness, to find the light within the shadows, to appreciate the power of resilience. The silence he had once feared had given birth to a new song, a song that celebrated not just success, but the bittersweet beauty of life's complexities, the strength forged in the fires of adversity, the unwavering spirit of the human heart.

He allowed himself a small smile. He was not the same person who had started his journey, the shy, uncertain boy who had dreamt of becoming a singer. He had become something more, something stronger, something deeper. The echoes of silence no longer haunted him. They had become a part of him, a testament to the long, arduous journey of self-discovery, a constant reminder of the lessons he'd learned, the battles he'd fought, and the peace he had finally found. The melody of his life, once shattered and discordant, was now a rich tapestry of sound, woven with threads of resilience, hope, and a profound understanding of the human experience.

The city lights seemed brighter now, less overwhelming, less alien. He felt a sense of calm settle over him, a quiet acceptance of the intricate dance of loss and gain, of sorrow and joy, that made up the rhythm of life. He had found his voice, not just as a singer, but as a man, a voice that resonated with the truth of his journey, a voice that spoke of the enduring power of the human spirit.

He closed his eyes, the city lights painting shimmering patterns on his eyelids. The rain had stopped, the storm within had subsided, leaving behind a quiet stillness, a sense of profound peace. He wasn't afraid of the future anymore. He knew that life would continue to throw its challenges, its surprises, its losses. But he also knew that he possessed the strength, the resilience, the understanding to face whatever came his way. The music would continue, the melody would evolve, and he, the architect of his own life, would continue to compose his own symphony, a beautiful, complex, and ultimately, triumphant song.

The silence was no longer an echo of loss. It was the quiet hum of acceptance, the gentle resonance of a life lived fully, authentically, and with a heart that, though wounded, continued to sing. The echoes of silence had become the prelude to a new dawn, a new song, a new beginning. He was ready. He was finally, truly, ready. The acceptance was not a surrender, but a powerful affirmation, a testament to the indomitable human spirit that could transform pain into strength, loss into wisdom, and silence into a beautiful, haunting melody. The journey had been brutal, but the melody of his life, once shattered, was now a symphony of self-discovery, a testament to the enduring power of the human heart. And that, he realized, was a victory far greater than any award, any accolade, any worldly success. This was his true triumph. His heart, once wounded, was not just singing again. It was soaring.

The Weight of Silence

The emptiness in the penthouse, once a gaping maw of regret, began to fill with a quieter kind of presence. It wasn't the boisterous applause of stadiums, nor the frantic flash of cameras. It was the subtle hum of acceptance, a quiet understanding that settled over him like the gentle fall of snow. He found himself drawn to the old, worn leather-bound books his grandfather had left him, stories of lives lived and battles fought, victories and defeats etched onto yellowed pages. In those tales, he found a strange comfort, a sense of kinship with characters who had faced their own demons, their own silences.

One evening, exploring a dusty box in the attic, he unearthed a worn cassette tape, labeled simply "Sakshi." He hesitated, his hand hovering over the player. The memories threatened to overwhelm him, a tidal wave of bittersweet longing. He knew he shouldn't play it. He hadn't listened to it in years, fearing the flood of emotions it would unleash. But a strange curiosity, a need to confront the past, propelled his hand forward.

The hiss of the tape filled the quiet room, followed by Sakshi's voice, clear and bright, yet tinged with a youthful uncertainty. It was a recording of a song they'd sung together, years ago, in a small park under the dappled shade of ancient trees. Her laughter, light and carefree, filled the space, a stark contrast to the heavy silence of his present. He closed his eyes, letting the melody wash over him, remembering the shy smiles, the stolen glances, the hesitant touch of hands.

The song ended, leaving a silence that was strangely peaceful. He felt no overwhelming sorrow, no agonizing regret. Instead, there was a sense of closure, a quiet understanding. He had made his choice, a choice that had led him down a path of incredible success, but at a significant cost. He'd sacrificed his personal life to achieve his dreams. Now he accepted that decision, not with resignation, but with a quiet dignity.

He spent the following weeks immersed in a different kind of music. He delved into the world of classical composition, finding solace in the intricate harmonies and complex melodies. The raw emotion that had previously fueled his pop songs now found a different outlet, a more refined, nuanced expression. He began composing pieces that mirrored his journey, the struggle, the pain, the quiet triumph. His music became a reflection of his inner world, a tapestry woven with threads of both darkness and light.

He started attending local community events, playing his compositions in small, intimate settings. He wasn't seeking fame or fortune, but something more profound – connection. He played for people who didn't know his name, who hadn't witnessed his meteoric rise to stardom. He played for the simple joy of sharing his music, of communicating his emotions through the universal language of melody.

His encounters with these people were unexpectedly nourishing. He listened to their stories, their struggles, their triumphs. He found kinship in their shared humanity, a reminder that despite the vast differences in their experiences, they all carried the weight of their own silences, their own unspoken stories. He learned from them, understanding that his own journey was not unique, his pain not singular.

One night, after a small concert in a local library, an elderly woman approached him. Her eyes, filled with a lifetime of wisdom, held a depth that resonated with his own. She didn't ask about his fame, his awards, or his chart-topping hits. Instead, she spoke to him about the music, the emotions it conveyed, the vulnerability it exposed. Her words were simple, yet profoundly insightful. She told him that the true measure of an artist wasn't the size of the crowd, but the depth of the connection made.

Her words were a revelation, a confirmation of the path he had unknowingly chosen. He had spent years chasing external validation, the roar of the crowd, the accolades of critics. He had sought recognition in the applause, in the bright lights, in the fleeting adoration of fans. Now, he realized that true fulfillment came not from the outside world, but from within. The silence he had once dreaded, the emptiness he had tried to fill with fame and fortune, now held a different kind of resonance – the quiet hum of self-acceptance, the gentle rhythm of inner peace.

His music began to reflect this newfound serenity, a shift that his listeners readily perceived. The raw, emotional intensity remained, but now it was tempered with a profound sense of peace, a quiet confidence born from self-acceptance. He was no longer seeking to prove anything to the world. He was simply sharing his truth, his journey, his heart.

He started volunteering at a local music school, teaching young aspiring musicians the same skills that had propelled him to success. He shared not just his technical knowledge, but also the wisdom he had gleaned from his own experiences – the importance of perseverance, the value of resilience, and the strength found in vulnerability. He saw his own past in their hopeful, wide eyes, their eagerness to share their own musical voices.

He continued to perform, but the focus shifted. The large stadiums were replaced by smaller venues, intimate gatherings, and the occasional charity event. His audience grew smaller, but their connection deepened. He found true joy in the shared experience, the collective breath held during a poignant melody, the collective sigh at the conclusion of a moving piece.

One day, he received a letter, an unexpected correspondence from Sakshi. It wasn't a declaration of love or a plea for reconciliation. It was a simple, heartfelt message of support, encouragement, and admiration for his music, his journey, and the man he had become. Reading her words, he felt a profound sense of peace. There was no bitterness, no lingering regret. Their paths had diverged, but their lives had remained intertwined in the fabric of his memories, the memories that had shaped his music, his character, and his understanding of himself.

The echoes of silence were no longer haunting, but a melody in themselves, a symphony of self-acceptance and a quiet understanding of life's complexities. The weight of the past, once a crushing burden, had been transmuted into a source of strength, shaping him into the artist he had always been destined to be. He had reached the pinnacle of his career, achieved his wildest dreams, and yet, he realized, true success lay not in the applause of the world, but in the quiet resonance of his own heart, finally at peace with its own song. The journey had been long and arduous, filled with challenges and sacrifices. But in the end, it was the quiet moments, the unspoken understandings, the silences filled with the gentle hum of acceptance that had truly defined his journey and led him to a quiet, profound, and ultimately fulfilling sense of wholeness. He was finally home. He was finally free.

A New Beginning

The scent of old paper and leather still clung to his fingers, a lingering fragrance of the countless hours spent lost within the pages of his grandfather's books. The penthouse, once a stark symbol of his lonely success, now felt... different. It wasn't just the absence of the clamorous crowds, the flashing lights, or the echoing silence. It was something deeper, a subtle shift in the very atmosphere of the place, a feeling of stillness infused with a quiet, persistent energy. He'd finally found a quiet peace, a stillness that was not emptiness, but a fullness born of acceptance.

He stood by the window, the city sprawling beneath him like a vast, glittering tapestry woven with a million different lives. The lights twinkled, a million tiny sparks against the velvet backdrop of the night, each one representing a story untold, a journey yet to unfold. He thought of Sakshi, a bittersweet ache lingering in his chest. The memory of her smile, the sound of her laughter, were etched into his soul, a constant, gentle reminder of the love he'd never fully grasped, the chance he'd let slip away in the relentless pursuit of his dream. But the regret, once a gnawing presence, now felt...softer. More like a worn, comfortable stone, smooth from years of handling, a testament to the lessons learned, the sacrifices made.

He poured himself a glass of whiskey, the amber liquid catching the light as he swirled it gently in the glass. The taste was smooth, familiar, a comforting ritual in the quiet solitude of his evening. He raised the glass in a silent toast, not to success, not to fame, but to the journey itself, the winding, unpredictable path that had led him to this moment, this quiet peace. He had climbed the highest mountain, reached the pinnacle of his ambition, yet the summit offered not just breathtaking views but a profound perspective. The view from the top was far more than just the sparkling panorama below; it was the understanding that the journey itself, with all its challenges and triumphs, had been the most enriching part of his life.

He picked up a worn photograph from his desk, a picture of him as a boy, his face hidden behind a shy smile. He remembered the taunts, the loneliness, the quiet desperation that had fueled his ambition. That boy, with his quiet demeanor and hidden dreams, was still a part of him, a foundation upon which his current self had been built. He was a different person now, shaped by experience, honed by hardship, his vulnerabilities now a source of strength. The boy who once hid in the shadows now stood bathed in the light of the world's stage.

He thought of his parents, their unwavering support, their faith in him, even when he doubted himself. Their love had been his anchor, the silent force that had propelled him forward, even when he was teetering on the brink of giving up. He felt a wave of gratitude wash over him, a poignant recognition of their sacrifice, their silent dedication. Their love had shaped him, taught him resilience, given him the strength to endure. He had been so focused on the distant goal, that he had failed to fully appreciate their constant support along the way.

The memory of his college years surfaced – the late-night rehearsals, the nervous energy before performances, the fleeting connections and deeper bonds he had forged. He remembered the girls, each one a unique experience, each encounter adding a new layer to his understanding of himself, of relationships, of the complex tapestry of human connection. He'd loved, and lost, and learned from each relationship, growing and evolving with every experience.

He considered the path not taken, the quiet life he might have lived, the love he might have found, if he had chosen differently. But there was no regret in his heart, only a quiet acceptance. He had chosen his path, and it had led him to a place of unexpected tranquility. It wasn't the life he had envisioned as a boy, but it was a life filled with a different kind of fulfillment, a contentment that went beyond the accolades and the applause. He was at peace with his choices, knowing that every decision, every sacrifice, had led him to this place of quiet understanding, this acceptance of self, this quiet symphony of his own making.

He opened one of his grandfather's books, the pages yellowed and brittle with age. He ran his fingers across the embossed lettering, feeling the texture of the aged leather, the weight of history contained within its pages. He opened it to a random page, his eyes falling upon a passage about resilience and acceptance, a tale of a journey that had ended, not with a grand flourish, but with a quiet understanding of life's complexities. The words resonated with him, a mirror reflecting his own journey, his own hard-won peace.

His story wasn't over, not really. It was simply reaching a quiet pause, a moment of reflection before the next chapter began. The echoes of silence he had once feared were now the melody of his life, a symphony woven from the threads of hardship and triumph, a testament to his resilience and to the quiet strength that lay within. The applause of the stadiums had faded, the flashbulbs no longer blinded him, but the quiet hum of his own heart, finally at peace, was a more profound music, a symphony of self-acceptance. The journey had led him here, to a place of quiet contentment, and yet, it also felt like the beginning of something new. The world still beckoned, with its endless possibilities, its untold stories. He was ready. He had reached the quiet peak of his musical journey, but life, in all its boundless wonder, waited for him at the foot of the next mountain, a promise of new adventures, new challenges, and, perhaps, even a different melody altogether. The song wasn't ending; it was simply evolving into something new, something yet to be written.

The night was deep, the city lights a constant hum below. He closed the old book gently, a soft sigh escaping his lips. He was home. But this home was not a destination, but a base camp, a place to rest before embarking on the next great adventure. The journey had taught him the value of solitude, the quiet strength of self-acceptance, and the profound beauty of life's silences. It was a journey that was far from finished, and he was ready to face whatever came next, not with the fierce ambition of his youth, but with the quiet confidence born of experience and the unwavering belief in the power of his own song. The echoes of silence, once a source of fear, were now the quiet hum of his own heart, a constant reminder of the long and arduous, yet ultimately fulfilling journey that had brought him to this place of serene acceptance. And as he drifted to sleep, the city lights whispered promises of a new dawn, a new beginning. A new song, yet to be sung.

www.ingramcontent.com/pod-product-compliance
Lightning Source LLC
Chambersburg PA
CBHW031429210526
45464CB00005B/2125